THE ECONOMIC
BASIS

THE ECONOMIC BASIS

OF A

DURABLE PEACE

by

J. E. MEADE

BASIS BOOKS
by arrangement with
GEORGE ALLEN & UNWIN LTD
London 1940

BASIS BOOKS

is a cheap edition venture organized by The Phoenix Book Company. Subscribers to Basic Books contract to receive certain books named in advance at monthly intervals and obtain them, by virtue of their contract, at low prices. *The Economic Basis of a Durable Peace* is the seventh of the Basis Books programme, and is sold to members only.

Contents

Chapter I

INTRODUCTORY

THE object of this book is to discuss the economic basis upon which a new international order may be built. In the circumstances of the moment, before the issue of the present conflict can be foreseen, it is impossible to discuss in detail the economic terms of a peace settlement. For it is still unknown what will be the political conditions when the time comes to reach a settlement, what countries will be involved in such a settlement, or how long and how far the economic wastes of war will have proceeded. Nevertheless, there are certain general principles which it is useful to discuss in spite of these many unknown factors.

It is no part of the purpose of this book to discuss the political terms of a peace settlement; but there are certain assumptions which must be made in order to make possible a useful discussion of the economic questions which are involved. Without some form of International Organization no international regulation of economic affairs is possible; and, as the arguments in the following chapters demonstrate, it is doubtful whether the economic bases of an International Organization

9   A*

can be firmly laid unless the Member States which constitute it restrict their freedom of national action in the economic sphere and grant corresponding powers of economic decision to the appropriate organs of the International Organization. These powers would clearly be concerned with international monetary relations and with international movements of commodity trade, of capital and of population.

It is, therefore, assumed for the purposes of this book that after the peace settlement some International Organization is in existence— whether this organization takes the form of the present or a revised League of Nations, or, for example, of a Federated Union of previously independent states; and it is further assumed that the Member States, which join together to form this International Organization, hand over certain economic questions for decision and administration by a duly constituted International Authority set up under the terms of the International Organization.

The International Organization will not necessarily be universal in scope, so that the problem arises of discussing the economic relations not only between the Member States themselves, but also between the Member States on the one hand and the non-member states on the other. It is, however, assumed that the International Organization either has a wide membership from the outset or else is especially designed so that its membership may be widely extended in the future. For this reason it is necessary to discuss the economic relations between Member States with widely different economic structures and policies; and in fact the organization of just and efficient economic relations between widely divergent economic systems forms one of the main themes of the following chapters.

It is probable that the main purposes of the International Organization will be military and political, in order to prevent conflicts among the Member States, or between the Member States and non-member states. Nevertheless, important economic considerations arise in the formation of the International Organization. In the first place, to a certain extent, the causes of international conflicts are economic in character; and for this reason only an International Organization which is based upon a stable, just, and efficient economic foundation can hope to succeed in its primary political tasks. But, in the second place, the International Organization will undoubtedly have as important subsidiary objectives the promotion of human welfare in various other ways, to help in the freeing of men's minds and bodies from ignorance, poverty, disease and hatred. For the purpose of raising standards of living the economic powers and policy of the International Organization must be wisely determined.

It is probable that economic motives have

been exaggerated as causes of war, at least in modern conditions. A purely economic cause of war could be said to exist only if a war was undertaken because the probable economic gains which were expected from a military conquest were reckoned to outbalance the probable economic cost of waging the war. In modern conditions the cost of a war of any magnitude is so great that it is doubtful whether it could in any case be made actually to pay economically. This does not mean that no economic advantages are to be gained by a costless war or through a bloodless diplomatic victory.

It is perhaps sufficient here merely to enumerate a few ways in which such action may bring economic gain. A particular territory may be closed as a market against a particular state through tariffs or other trade restrictions; and the economic disadvantages to the state in question will be particularly great if these trade restrictions discriminate against her and favour her closest competitors. Conquest of such a territory and removal of these trade restrictions may thus expand the markets for the particular state's exports. In a similar manner restrictions —particularly if they are of a discriminatory character—upon the export of essential commodities may work to the disadvantage of a country, which must of necessity import its supplies of such commodities. Such restrictions may take the form not only of direct export duties but also of monopolistic restriction schemes, which are devised to diminish supplies and to raise prices of an essential commodity; for by this means the producers in the exporting country or colony may be able to make monopoly profits at the expense of consumers in the importing country. In this case conquest of the territory in question may enable the importing country to remove a real obstacle to the development of its economic welfare.

Similar considerations may apply to restrictions imposed upon international capital movements or upon international migration of labour. Political control over, or influence in, a particular territory may enable a state to obtain concessions for certain types of capital development on preferential terms for its own nationals. Other states may then wish to dispute this political influence in order to share in the possibilities of the territory in question as a field for profitable capital investment. Or, again, a country in which there is already a relatively heavy pressure of population upon the available natural resources and capital equipment may only with difficulty find employment for a growing population within its own territory. If other territories are closed to its emigrants, it may find some economic advantage by obtaining political control over possible fields for immigration.

In all these ways—by breaking down restrictions which hamper its export or import trade, or which limit the possible fields of capital investment or of labour migration—a particular nation may stand to gain economically from a successful war, if the war itself is not too costly. Moreover, the economic gain so obtained may take the form not merely of removing restrictions which have previously been placed against the trade or the capital or labour of the victorious state, but also of erecting such restrictions in the newly-acquired territories to the advantage of the victors and to the disadvantage of the vanquished. In some cases, for reasons of this kind, direct economic motives may be at least a contributory factor in the causation of a war.

In Japan the economic factor has been important. For in this case a rapidly growing population found its access to export markets and to possible fields for emigration severely restricted; and at the same time there was already a considerable pressure of population within a territory which needed to import a large variety of essential commodities. But in other cases vast expenditure on armaments have been incurred in peace time, and large-scale economic disruption and destruction has been faced in war time, for objectives which, from the strictly economic point of view, might make a slight but by no means decisive change in the country's standard of living.

But this does not prove that economic factors have not *indirectly* played a really important part in the failure to maintain peace. Economic events have widespread social and psychological consequences. The economic injustice of a particular trade preference, the removal of which would in fact make but a slight economic difference to anyone's standard of living, may nevertheless cause widespread national resentment. Poverty, and in particular the fall from comfort to poverty in a period of national economic collapse, breeds a state of mind in which military adventures appear more attractive than would otherwise be the case. The same is true of economic uncertainty of every kind and of unemployment in particular, which may lead to a sullen resentment that finds expression—for purely irrational reasons—against the national enemies. Great inequalities of income between the classes within a state or between the inhabitants of different countries may have similar psychological effects.

For example, two economic events of first-rate importance in Germany—namely the great inflation of 1923 and the great depression from 1929 to 1933—played a substantial, if indirect, part in causing the breakdown of the last peace. The inflation impoverished the middle class in Germany and produced a feeling of unjustified economic calamity at least in that section of the population. The widespread unemployment and poverty which was caused in the working class and the middle class by the post-1929 depression greatly extended this feeling. These two events formed the economic conditions in which the whole political and "ideological" structure of Germany was reshaped.

The evil effects of the great depression were as worldwide as the depression itself. In nearly every country there occurred to a lesser or greater degree a sudden decline in employment and in income, due largely to technical economic factors of the nature of which the vast majority of men were completely ignorant; and this aroused a widespread state of mind which was most inimical to the reasonable development of international organization precisely at a time when some years of uneventful stability might decisively have strengthened the peace system created after 1918.

The great depression had, moreover, a rather more direct influence upon international relations. When a slump occurs within any country there are, broadly speaking, two types of policy which may be adopted to overcome the general decline in the demand for goods and services. In the first place, by means of protective tariffs and import quotas, by export subsidies of a disguised or open character, by cutting wage-costs in the industries producing for export, and by an unjustifiable depreciation of the national currency designed to reduce prices in foreign markets, measures may be taken to expand a particular nation's markets at the expense of other nations.

Such measures were adopted on a large scale to meet the post-1929 depression. Not only were they largely ineffective—for in most cases they led to counterbalancing retaliatory measures on the part of the nations whose markets were threatened—but they naturally led to a rapid deterioration in international political relations.

The second main method of meeting a general slump is for each nation to rely primarily upon the re-expansion of its internal demand for goods and services by a monetary and economic policy designed to restore money incomes. Various measures may be taken for this purpose. The banks, by increasing the supplies of money and by reducing interest rates, may induce producers to borrow fresh funds for expenditure on new capital developments. The state and other public authorities may support this "easy money" policy by borrowing fresh funds to spend on various schemes of public construction. These new streams of money expenditure upon capital construction will raise employment, wages and profits in the construction industries. This in turn will lead to the expenditure of some part of the increased incomes upon various goods required for current consumption. Employment, wages and profits will rise in the industries producing consumption goods. This in turn will lead to further increases in expenditure on consumption goods; and the consequent restoration of profits will re-stimulate private capital construction.[1] Such a policy has the advantage that it will help to increase the demand in the nation which practises it not only for home-produced goods but also for foreign-produced imports; and thus it positively eases for other nations that search for markets which is the most common feature of a widespread depression. It is true that this may lead to an unbalanced excess of imports into any particular nation which is alone adopting such a policy of internal "reflation," and that this danger may have to be met by special protective measures; but if the generality of nations simultaneously adopt policies of internal expansion each individual nation will discover that its external markets are expanding as quickly as its own demand for imports. The moral may, therefore, safely be drawn that the adoption of proper principles of policy to meet trade depressions is one of the chief economic bases of a durable peace.[2]

In all these ways economic factors may con-

[1] For a more detailed description of the various processes cf. J. E. Meade: *An Introduction to Economic Analysis and Policy*, Part I, and for a suggested scheme for the direct stimulation of expenditure upon current consumption cf. J. E. Meade: *Consumers' Credits and Unemployment*.

[2] In addition to the direct and indirect economic causes of war which have been mentioned above, there is another class of factors which are semi-economic and semi-military. Nations seek control of sources of supply of essential commodities in order to make themselves more nearly self-sufficient in case of war; and the search for control over such commodities may provide a semi-military, semi-economic reason for conflict.

tribute, directly and indirectly, to the causation of international conflicts. In order to reduce their potency to a minimum it is desirable to build an efficient and a just international economic order. But such an economic order is desirable—perhaps primarily—in and for itself, because it is an instrument for raising the standard of living. It is largely with this latter object in mind that the following chapters have been written; but as the foregoing remarks make clear, prosperity and peace should give each other mutual support in the development of better international relations.

Chapter II

LIBERAL AND PLANNED ECONOMIES

THE problem of determining the basic principles for a just and efficient international economic organization has been greatly complicated in recent years by the growing diversity of economic structures in the various national states. In the later years of the nineteenth century and in the early years of the twentieth century before the war of 1914–18 the majority of countries based their economic systems upon the same essential pattern. Property was privately owned and production was privately managed. The forces of competitive economic markets were allowed to determine prices, output, employment and wages. State intervention and regulation existed to a limited extent, and in some spheres—such as that of public supervision of social welfare— was rapidly growing; but even in these cases state regulation remained rather an exception which modified the general rule of free market conditions and individualistic competition. In international relations the nations traded upon the basis of a common monetary gold standard. In the case of so important a country as the

United Kingdom the principle of economic *laissez-faire* was applied to international trade through the adoption of a commercial policy of Free Trade; in many other countries tariffs were comparatively low; and the recent paraphernalia of import quotas, exchange controls, clearing agreements, and similar devices for the strict regulation of foreign trade were conspicuous only by their absence. Moreover, international capital movements and international migration of labour were much less restricted than in recent years. If in such conditions it had been decided to construct an International Organization, the economic bases would normally and naturally have been those of economic liberalism. The Organization itself might have been built soundly upon a common currency and upon the freedom of movement of trade, of capital and of labour between the various Member States, each of which would itself have adopted an internal policy essentially of economic *laissez-faire*.

But in recent years conditions have been very different. There still remain important states whose recent peace-time economies have been based upon liberal individualistic principles. But even in these cases the superstructure of state regulation imposed upon the competitive econo-nomic basis has been growing rapidly; and there have at the same time been very important divergences of economic and monetary policy in these essentially liberal economies. Simultaneously there have existed economic systems in which state control and management have become the basic economic principle; of these the most striking example is the Union of Soviet Socialist Republics where property is state owned, industries are state managed, prices and output are centrally planned, and foreign trade forms a state monopoly. No hard and fast dividing line can be drawn between the "liberal" and the "planned" economies; for, in fact, there is the possibility of an almost infinite number of combinations of economic freedom and of state control of various kinds, for various purposes and of various degrees of severity. Moreover, the essentially "planned" economies vary greatly in the political, social and economic objectives of their planning and in the methods of state regulation which are chosen for this purpose.

The variety of existing economic structures and policies is so significant for the arguments of this book that it is important to illustrate the principal divergences which have recently developed. The United Kingdom, France and the United States of America may all be taken as examples of important states whose peace-time economies have remained essentially liberal. On the whole production and trade have been left to private enterprise, and the greater part of industrial capital and of agricultural land has remained in private ownership. In the main prices, profits, wages and output have been left to the determination of free market forces. Dealings with other countries involving foreign exchange transactions have been uncontrolled. Foreign trade has been subject to various restrictions; but, with the exception of France, the restrictions have taken the form mainly of import duties and only to a minor extent of the more rigid and severe form of quantitative control by means of import quotas.

While this essential structure remains in common to the liberal economies, there have been many instances of state intervention and of partial "planning" for particular industries. In particular state control of wages and of hours of work, control of agricultural prices and production, and, above all, the control of foreign trade for protective purposes have grown rapidly in recent years. In the United Kingdom and France war controls have been imposed over profits, prices, production and employment; and it is impossible to foretell to what extent these controls may be maintained in a modified form as permanent peace measures.

In all the "liberal" economies various experiments in financial and economic intervention by the state had been tried between 1929 and 1939 to reduce the severity of the unemployment problem which arose as a result of the great depression. It is in respect of these various "anti-slump" measures that the economic policies of the liberal economies have displayed their most marked divergences; and, as will be seen in the two following chapters, divergences of this kind raise most important problems for the formation of an efficient International Organization.[1]

The United Kingdom met the forces of the great depression by abandoning the gold standard and depreciating the exchange value of the pound in 1931, as a result of the existing strain on her balance of payments and the consequent heavy losses of gold. At the same time a general tariff was introduced to protect British markets from foreign competition; and in 1932 the Ottawa agreements introduced the principles of imperial preference into this tariff structure. An internal policy of monetary expansion was adopted, which from 1932 onwards was very successful in providing cheap and plentiful supplies of money for producers. But at the same time the state did not indulge in any programme of expenditure on public works to promote the recovery; and in fact the budget was strictly balanced after 1931 until the large-scale programme of rearmament was developed in 1937.

[1] In considering the following short description of the various "anti-slump" policies adopted in the United Kingdom, France and the United States after 1929, the reader should bear in mind the distinction mentioned in the previous chapter between policies which are designed to expand the national market at the expense of the markets of other countries and policies of internal expansion which help incidentally to expand the markets for the goods of other countries as well.

This combination of protection and of cheap money led to a vigorous economic recovery.

The United Kingdom did not embark on any very extensive schemes of internal economic planning or control except in the case of agriculture, in which various marketing schemes—based usually upon the protection of the home market—were devised to control agricultural prices and output and to extend home production. In France and the United States, however, less orthodox experiments were tried. In France at first the depression was met by a stern adherence to the gold standard and by a severe deflation of prices, incomes and costs, which lasted until 1936, although both the United Kingdom and the United States had by then depreciated their currencies and had adopted reflationary internal monetary policies.

In 1936, however, this policy was dramatically changed with the inception of the "Blum" experiment. Hours of work were restricted to forty a week in order to reduce unemployment, and hourly wage-rates were raised to prevent the shorter hours of work from leading to a reduction in total wage incomes and so in the total demand of wage-earners for goods and services. The consequent rise in money costs and prices necessitated the abandonment of the gold standard and the depreciation of the exchange value of the franc. This policy was combined with a programme of state expenditure upon public works financed by means of a growing budget deficit. There was, however, a continued export of monetary capital by speculators who foresaw the successive depreciations in the exchange value of the franc; and at the same time the rapid rise in internal costs and prices increased the internal demand for cash. For these reasons the internal supply of money remained comparatively scarce, and the cost of borrowing remained high. The high cost of borrowing combined with the rapid rise in wage costs prevented the success of the experiment. In fact it was not fully realized that for every penny by which the wage-earner's purchasing power is increased through higher hourly wage rates, the wage costs of production are raised by an identical penny.

In the United States of America a policy of reducing the costs of borrowing by means of an expansion in monetary supplies was adopted in the early years of the great depression. But with the inception of the "New Deal" in 1933 a great variety of different experiments in state intervention was started in order to reform certain economic and social evils and to promote recovery from the depression. In a number of cases these experiments have been the subject of rapid changes in substance and, particularly, in administrative form; but many of the basic principles of the New Deal have remained consistently unchanged.

Thus from the inception of the New Deal the same monetary and budgetary policy has been adopted. In order to stimulate monetary expenditure and so economic activity in general, plentiful and cheap monetary supplies have been provided; and public expenditure on relief and recovery has been maintained at a high level and has been financed by means of government borrowing. A consistent objective of the New Deal has been to raise wage rates and to reduce hours of work, in order to diminish unemployment by raising wage-earners' purchasing power and by spreading the available amount of work; but this policy has been executed by varying administrative devices, first through the regulation of industry by the National Recovery Administration and later by the application of the Fair Labour Standards Act of 1938. As in the case of France the increased wage rates have raised wage costs as well as wage-earners' incomes. Several other internal economic measures have been undertaken. By various devices the output of different agricultural products has been restricted in order to raise agricultural prices and incomes. An important scheme of social insurance for pensions and for unemployment benefit has been initiated. In a number of ways the market for stocks and shares has been subjected to state regulation.

In addition to these internal economic measures various acts of state policy profoundly modified economic relations with other states. In 1930 very high duties were imposed on imports, and in 1933 the exchange value of the dollar was depreciated.

27

These measures accentuated the already existing excess of monetary receipts from other countries in the balance of international payments of the United States, and thus intensified the existing drain of gold from other countries to the United States. From 1934 onwards, however, by means of its Trade Agreements Programme the United States negotiated a series of treaties for the general reduction of trade barriers, culminating in the Anglo-American Trade Agreement of 1938.

Germany and the Union of Soviet Socialist Republics may be taken as examples of states which in recent years have had essentially "planned" economic systems. Germany suffered very heavily from the great depression, largely as a result of the internal deflationary policy which was at first adopted to maintain the gold value of the mark. The strain upon the German balance of international payments was particularly severe as a result of many factors: the cessation of the foreign lending to Germany which had occurred between 1924 and 1929; the attempts on the part of foreign creditors to remove the capital which they had invested in Germany; the payment of reparations and of interest and sinking fund on foreign loans; and the rapid growth of import restrictions on manufactured products in Germany's former markets. But in 1933 with the advent to power of the National Socialists this policy of deflation gave place to one of vigorous and rapid reflation.

Heavy public expenditure was incurred on public works, such as the construction of motor-roads, and in particular on rearmament and on the promotion of industries which were desired for military reasons. These heavy expenditures were financed essentially by an expansion of monetary supplies through an appropriate banking policy.

This policy achieved remarkable success in the cure of unemployment, but led to a great extension of state control over the economic relations with other states. It was decided not to depreciate the exchange value of the mark from its previous official gold value, even though the internal expansion of purchasing power threatened to lead to a great excess of imports. To prevent this, and to protect home industries, imports were limited by quotas administered by import boards, and all foreign exchange dealings were subjected to strict regulation. At the same time various other measures, to which reference will be made in Chapter VII below, were adopted to expand export trade and to obtain the imports of raw materials which were necessary for the prosecution of the rearmament programme.

In other ways also the German programme was accompanied by a large extension of state control. In essence the system was devised not only to absorb the unemployed resources into work on rearmament and on other state projects, but also to divert much labour, capital and raw materials to such state purposes from civil uses. Wages and dividends were limited largely in order to prevent a rise in demand for current consumption goods. By controlling the issue of new stocks and shares on the capital market and by rationing the distribution of necessary raw materials, private enterprise was prevented from undertaking developments for civil purposes which were not deemed essential by the state. Not only were capital and raw materials rationed in this way, but a strict control was instituted over the labour market with the twofold object of increasing the total available supplies of labour and of diverting labour into the occupations which were considered essential for the state plan. To prevent the rise in prices and costs which would otherwise have resulted from the scarcity of productive resources in relation to the expanded monetary demands for goods and services, a strict control was instituted over commodity prices and over wage-rates.

In Germany the greater part of industrial and agricultural property remains in private ownership, and is managed by private enterprise, although a vast superstructure of state regulation and control has been built upon this basis. In the Union of Soviet Socialist Republics, on the other hand, practically all industrial property is both owned and managed by the state. According to a centrally determined plan prices, output and wage-rates are determined by the state, and are not influenced by the forces of competitive markets. This all-embracing control permits the state to determine the proportion of the national income which shall be withheld from wage-earners for the finance of the production of new capital equipment. The natural accompaniment of this internal economic system has been a complete state monopoly of foreign trade and of dealings in foreign exchange. By such a system of state ownership and planning it has been possible to abolish unemployment, to devote an abnormally large proportion of the national income to capital development, and to redistribute the national income more equally among the individual citizens.

A system of complete state socialism of this kind presents one important problem. In a liberal economic system the forces of competitive markets are permitted to determine the prices and outputs of the various alternative commodities which might be produced by the limited supplies of labour, capital and raw materials which are available for production. The prices which consumers offer in the competitive markets show the extent to which they desire additional supplies of the various commodities. The competitive demand on the part of the producers for labour, capital and raw materials fixes the wage, interest and raw material costs of production; and the search for profits ensures that these factors of production will be used in the industries in which the margin between costs of production and the prices offered by consumers is greatest. By these means flexibility is maintained in the economic system, and factors of production are attracted to produce those goods which the consumers most desire.

This system has another equally important, though less obvious, advantage. The determination in competitive markets of the costs of the various factors of production—labour, capital, land and raw materials—means that these costs will correspond to the relative scarcities of the various factors. The profit motive, displaying itself in the desire to reduce costs to a minimum, will lead to the substitution of less expensive for more expensive methods of production; and this will result in the use of technical methods of production which economize to the utmost those factors of production which are the most scarce.

These advantages do not accrue automatically in a system of complete state socialism, since prices both of the factors of production and of finished commodities are fixed by decree of the authorities. Nevertheless it is *possible* in a socialized economy to make such a use of the pricing system as to obtain these advantages from it. Consumers may be left free to determine the prices at which they will purchase the quantities of the various goods which are put on sale in the state shops. These prices can then be compared with the costs of producing the planned quantities of the various commodities, and the plan may be revised from time to time to increase the output of those commodities in which the margin between price and cost is greatest. By this means flexibility in following consumers' desires can be maintained.

The problem, however, remains of revising the planned prices of the factors of production upon which the costs of production of the various commodities is to be reckoned. This in turn is not impossible. To each of the socialized factories quantities of the various factors of production are offered for sale at certain prices. The managers of the various factories can be asked to reduce their costs of production wherever this is possible by substituting one factor for another to produce their planned output. If on the balance this threatens to lead to an excessive demand for one factor and to the under employment of the available supplies of another factor, the planned price of the former may be raised and of the latter may be lowered. By such means a costing system may be used to ensure that the most economical use is made of the available supplies of the factors of production.[1]

The above description of the problem of pricing and costing in a completely planned economy may at first sight appear irrelevant in a book on

[1] For a more detailed discussion of the problem of pricing and costing in a completely planned economy, see J. E. Meade: *Introduction to Economic Analysis and Policy*, Part II, Chapter viii.

the economic bases of peace. But this is not so. The problem of building an efficient International Organization in which both "liberal" and "planned" national economies may be included is a serious one; and as will become clear in later chapters of this book the question turns partly upon the extent to which the prices determined in the planned economy may be used for the same purposes as the prices of a liberal competitive economy. To answer this question, some understanding of the principles of pricing in the two systems is essential.

The foregoing description of recent economic policies in various countries may have served to show two things; first, the extent to which economic policies can diverge, and have in fact diverged, even in the economies whose basic principles remain liberal; and, secondly, the wide essential differences which exist between the "liberal" and the "planned" economies. On what economic principles, then, is an efficient and just International Organization to be built? Should the Organization be restricted to the countries with liberal economies and to those which are willing hereafter to adopt a liberal economic system? It might be relatively easy to devise the basic economic principles for such an organization, although even in this case the wide divergences which have existed between the economic policies of the various liberal economies would raise many problems, as will become clear in the following chapters. Should the economic powers of the International Authority be so extensive as to make it possible to impose from the centre the same uniform pattern of economic planning for all the states which became members of the International Organization?

There are two reasons why neither of these drastic solutions appears to be desirable. In the first place, the states which might otherwise be willing to form an International Organization, would quite possibly be unwilling to adopt a uniform pattern of economic structure, whether of a liberal kind or of a particular variety of planned economy. But, secondly, it is questionable whether such uniformity would be desirable even if it were possible. There is no general agreement among economists or among statesmen as to which particular variety of economic system is the best. The world has recently passed through a period of diverse economic experiments in different countries. Each experiment has shown some weaknesses and some strengths; but it is doubtful if any single system has yet been devised which presents the best possible solution for all the major economic problems of all the countries. Much may still, perhaps, be learned from the continuation of national economic experiments, which will allow each nation to learn from the successes and failures of others. But must an International Organization which is built upon widely divergent national economic systems be too loose to work efficiently or to preserve a just economic balance between the constituent parts? Can *any* connecting economic principles be found which are of general application to all economic systems and which can therefore form the basis of an International Organization comprising both "planned" and "liberal" economies? It is to the solution of these problems that the remaining chapters are devoted.

Chapter III

AN INTERNATIONAL CURRENCY

WE may start our more detailed discussion of the economic aspects of the International Organization with the question of the monetary relations between the Member States; and in this connection the first task is to examine the proposal that the Member States should adopt a common international currency.

In many respects the institution of an international currency would have the same results as the return of the Member States to the gold standard. For as long as a freely operating gold standard existed, the large number of states which had fixed the gold value of their currencies were able freely to make payments to each other by means of shipments of gold; and since a certain weight of gold represented a determinate value in the currency of each of the various countries, gold performed many of the functions of an international currency. It is, therefore, of importance to examine the working of the gold standard as a basis for the discussion of an international currency.

A country may be said to adhere to a freely operating gold standard if (i) its monetary

37

authorities have taken steps to fix the value of the national currency unit—the pound, the dollar or the franc—in terms of gold, and if (ii) gold may be freely imported and exported. The former of these two conditions—the fixing of the gold value of the national currency—can be achieved in various ways, of which two examples may be given. If gold coins of a certain weight of gold are the legal tender currency of a country, and if individuals are free both to have gold minted into these coins and also to melt gold coin for export or for industrial purposes, the value of the national monetary unit will be maintained at the value of its legal gold content. But a country can adhere to a gold standard without possessing a circulation of gold coins. It is possible, for example, for the legal tender currency of the country to take the form of the notes issued by the Central Bank of the country. But if the Central Bank keeps a reserve of gold against its note issue and is under a legal obligation to purchase and sell gold freely at a fixed price in exchange for its notes, the gold value of the country's monetary unit will be effectively fixed.

The immediate result of the fixation of the gold value of a number of national currencies and of the freedom of movement of gold between the nations in question is that the rate of exchange between their currencies is fixed. Suppose for example that a certain quantity of gold has the fixed value of $5 notes in the United States and of a £1 note in the United Kingdom, and that gold can be freely shipped between these two countries. The value of exchange between the pound and the dollar will be fixed practically at £1 == $5. For no Englishman will give much more than £1 in notes for $5 notes, if he can obtain $5 by shipping £1 worth of gold from the United Kingdom. Similarly no American will accept much less than £1 for $5 notes if he can ship $5 worth of gold from the United States to obtain £1 in notes in the United Kingdom.[1]

The importance of the gold standard lies in the fact that it provides an automatic method of adjusting the balance of international payments between the nations which adhere to it. Suppose, for example, that—for reasons which will be discussed in later sections of this chapter—the English demand for American goods increases in such a way that the United Kingdom has an excess of payments to make to the United States. The pound price of dollars will tend to rise in view of the excessive demand for dollars to finance the additional purchases of American goods. But if Englishmen can obtain dollars at the old rate by purchasing gold in the United Kingdom and exporting it to the United States, the additional payments will be financed in this way.

[1] The rate of exchange can vary slightly within certain "gold points" which depend upon the various costs of shipping gold. For a more detailed description and discussion of the mechanism of the gold standard, see J. E. Meade, *An Introduction to Economic Analysis and Policy*, Part V, Chapter ii.

This shipment of gold will have a double effect. It will reduce monetary reserves in the United Kingdom and will increase such reserves in the United States. The loss of gold reserves will cause the monetary authorities in the United Kingdom to restrict supplies of money. The scarcity of money will reduce the general level of money expenditure, of money incomes, of money prices, and of money costs. At the same time money expenditure, incomes, prices, and costs will rise in the United States as a result of the inflow of monetary reserves there.

These changes will enable the balance of international payments of the United Kingdom to be brought back into equilibrium. For the fall in money incomes and prices in the United Kingdom will cause British expenditure on American goods to decline, both because the British have smaller incomes to spend and also because home-produced goods have become cheaper relatively to imports. For the opposite reasons the Americans will spend more on the products of the United Kingdom. For these reasons the United Kingdom's payments for imports will decline and her receipts from exports will rise, until the excess of payments over receipts in her balance of payments has disappeared. Such is the classical theory of the automatic readjustments brought about by the operation of the gold standard.[1]

[1] As will be seen in later passages of this chapter, in practice there are various economic frictions and obstacles which prevent so smooth a working of the monetary machinery.

To what extent and in what way would the operation of an International Currency differ from that of an international monetary standard, such as the gold standard? To answer this question a distinction must be drawn between the possible forms which an International Currency may take.

(1) Suppose that a number of countries are operating a gold standard on the basis of the free coinage of gold into national coins—the gold sovereign in the United Kingdom, the gold dollar in the United States, and the gold franc in France. These countries might all agree to mint coins of the same gold value and with the same name instead of minting their previous national coins. They would, in fact, agree to use the same monetary unit of account. But if their banking and monetary systems otherwise remained unaffected by the reform, the International Currency system would differ in no respect from the gold standard system based on the free minting of national gold coins—except in the convenience of having the same monetary unit of account for all countries.

(2) Suppose, secondly, that a number of countries are operating a gold standard, based on the legal obligation of the Central Bank of each individual country to buy and sell gold at a fixed price in terms of its note issue—the British pound note, the American dollar note, and the French franc note. These countries might then agree simply to use the same monetary unit of

account, so that each Central Bank should issue notes of the same name and of the same gold value. Again, this system would in no essential differ from that of the corresponding type of gold standard, except for the added convenience of having the same unit of account for monetary affairs in each country.

(3) A number of countries might, however, agree to set up a common International Bank, to take over the right of note issue from all the national Central Banks. These notes, which might or might not be backed by a central reserve of gold held by the International Bank, might form the only legal tender currency throughout the countries concerned. This would constitute in a full sense an International Currency, even though the national central banks retained all the functions of central banks except the right of issuing notes. Each national central bank could, for example, remain the banker for its own national government; and it might retain the power of influencing the rates of interest within its own national territory by raising or lowering the "bank rate" at which it was willing to grant additional credits or by expanding or contracting the supply of deposit money through the purchase or sale of securities.[1] But the operations of each

[1] When a Central Bank grants a loan or purchases securities it may pay for them by the creation of a new deposit account to the credit of the person or institution to whom the loan is made or from whom the securities have been purchased. This newly created deposit will probably be paid into an ordinary commercial bank,

42

Central Bank would now be subject to the condition that it must retain a sufficient reserve of the International Currency notes to meet any demands that may be made for such notes by the commercial banks or other persons or institutions which held deposits with it.

A system of this kind differs in two respects from an international gold standard. In the first place, in common with the two other forms of International Currency which we have just examined, it has the advantage that each country will be using the same monetary unit of account. But, secondly, this system allows for the constitution of an International Monetary Authority to control the total issue of the International Currency. In the case of the gold standard and of the two other forms of International Currency discussed above, the total monetary reserves of all the countries adhering to the system depend upon accidental circumstances affecting the gold mining industry and the demand for gold for non-monetary purposes. With an International Currency of the third type, the total monetary reserves available to the aggregate of Member

which will thus increase its monetary reserves held with the Central Bank. On the basis of these additional reserves the commercial bank may lend new money to its customers or invest new funds in securities thereby further increasing the supply of deposit money. Conversely, the recall of a loan or a sale of securities by a Central Bank will cause a reduction in the supply of deposit money. For a fuller description of this process, see J. E. Meade, *An Introduction to Economic Analysis and Policy*, Part I, Chapter iii.

States would be in the control of an International Authority.

This aspect of a fully developed International Currency is of great importance, and will be discussed in a later section of this chapter. At the moment it is necessary to realize that as an instrument for adjusting the balance of payments between the various Member States even a fully developed International Currency works in essentially the same way as the gold standard. If, for example, one particular state for one reason or another develops an excess of payments over receipts in its balance of international payments, the excess will be financed by an export of International Currency notes to the other states. This will cause a diminution in the supply of money in the state in question which should lead to a fall in money expenditures, incomes, prices and costs; and there should be a converse rise in money incomes and prices in the countries which are receiving additional International Currency notes. These movements should reduce the demand for imports by the state whose incomes and prices are falling as a result of the loss of monetary reserves, and should expand its exports to the states whose incomes are rising and whose products are become dearer as a result of the inflow of monetary reserves. By this means the equilibrium in the balance of international payments will be restored.

It is true that the Central Bank of the country

which is losing its reserves of International Currency notes may for a time maintain total national monetary supplies by expanding the internal supply of deposit money as fast as notes are exported. But this cannot last. For so long as money prices and incomes are maintained in this state, the excess of its payments to other states will continue and the export of International Currency notes will not slacken. Sooner or later this export of monetary reserves will threaten to deplete the reserves of the national Central Bank; and at this point the Central Bank must reduce the supply of deposit money and thus deflate incomes and prices, in order to maintain the convertibility of its deposits into the International Currency notes.

This mechanism of the gold standard or of an International Currency has certain clear advantages over the alternative system of independent national currencies, the rate of exchange between which is allowed to fluctuate. International trade is subject to one less risk and therefore to one less obstacle, if there is no fear of fluctuations in the rate of exchange between the various national moneys. Moreover, recent economic experience has shown that speculative movements of monetary funds from one currency to another are greatly encouraged by the prospect of possible changes in the rate of exchange between various currencies; and the flight of money from a currency which is expected to depreciate may seriously embarrass both the internal economic policy of that country and also the orderly development of international economic relations.

There are, however, equally weighty arguments against the institution of a single monetary circulation for a number of nations. It has already been seen that the operation of such a monetary system involves a reduction in money expenditure, money incomes, money prices, and money costs in any country which is subject to an external drain of its monetary reserves. But this process of general deflation does not necessarily operate smoothly and easily. The reduction in money expenditure on goods and services, resulting from an outflow of monetary reserves, may lead at first simply to a smaller volume of business turnover and so to reduced production and increased unemployment. If commodity prices are readily reduced as a result of increased competition among producers to serve the shrinking market for their products, and if money wage-rates fall rapidly as a result of increased competition for jobs among unemployed workers, the level of prices and costs may quickly fall to correspond to the lower level of monetary demand. If this happens, production and employment will be restored again to their previous level. No permanent harm will then have been done by the deflation; for real wages and real incomes will not have suffered, since money prices and the cost of living will have fallen simultaneously with money wages and other money incomes.

But in modern economic systems, and in particular in systems which are more or less "planned," there are likely to be considerable rigidities of money prices and costs which prevent an easy readjustment of this kind. For example, the prices of railway fares, of gas, electricity, water, and other public services, school fees, and the fees of other professional services are all likely to be conventionally fixed or to be regulated by legislative or administrative measures. Industrial cartels or agricultural marketing schemes, with or without official backing, may have fixed the prices of the commodities which they control, and these prices may be subject to relatively infrequent revision. Rents, insurance premiums, and similar payments may be rigidly fixed by long-term contracts. At the same time certain money costs of production are relatively rigid. Fixed interest on debt and rents for land and other property used for productive purposes remain fixed by long-term contracts. In particular money wage-rates are fixed by convention, by long-term bargains between Trade Unions and employers, by official wage boards, and by minimum wage legislation. In such conditions a general deflation of money expenditure and money income might lead to a considerable decline of production and employment, and trade would remain stagnant for a long time while prices and costs were adjusting themselves to the lower level.

In every modern economy there are at least some serious frictions of this kind. In order, therefore, that an International Currency system may work effectively, it is essential to ensure that no Member State is likely to be subjected to too prolonged or too serious a deflation. In past years the most serious deflationary pressures which have been imposed on countries adhering to the gold standard have been due to the development of widespread general trade depressions—such as the great post-1929 slump.[1]

Let us suppose that a general slump in state A leads to a fall in money expenditure and so in incomes and prices in A. This may have serious repercussions in state B. For A will spend less on

---

[1] There are those who hold (cf. C. Streit, *Union Now*) that the formation of an international economic system based upon free trade and a common currency would remove the threat of widespread trade depressions. It is not possible in this book to explain the reasons for believing that, even in such conditions, the various economic systems might still be threatened with serious depressions from time to time. Two considerations may, however, make this suggestion appear at least plausible. First, the great depression of 1929–32 started in the United States, which was by far the most important economic area organized on a basis of free trade and a common currency. Secondly, during the nineteenth century recurrent trade depressions occurred, when the majority of the most important countries adhered to a common international gold standard and when there were comparatively liberal conditions for international trade. For a more detailed examination of the problem of trade depressions, see J. E. Meade, *An Introduction to Economic Analysis and Policy*, Part I.

B's goods, as spendable incomes decline in A and as the prices of A's products decline below those of B. At the same time the citizens of B may be tempted to spend less on their own products and to import more from A, as the price of A's products decline. The depression will thus spread to B as expenditure on B's products is reduced; and during this process B's exports will be low and her imports high, so that B will have an excess of payments to make to other countries over her monetary receipts from other countries.

How could B meet this situation except by deflating her prices and money incomes to correspond with the lower level of prices and incomes in A? In the first place, B might impose a tariff or an import quota upon the purchase of goods from A, and by this means the excess of B's imports could be removed. Secondly, this excess of imports could be removed if B was able to depreciate the value of her money in terms of A's money, for, as will be seen in the next chapter, this will expand B's exports by reducing their price in A, and will restrict B's imports by raising their price in B. If, however, there is an International Currency and if at the same time—as will be suggested in Chapter V—the International Organization adopts a policy of free trade among the Member States, state B will be obliged to undertake an internal deflation of prices and incomes on the same scale as that which has been caused by the general trade depression in A.

Some countries have much more flexible systems of internal prices and costs than others; and in particular the "liberal" economies, which practice a *laissez-faire* economic policy, are likely to have fewer economic rigidities than the "planned" economies. The former may be able with relative ease to deflate their money costs as a method of meeting the fall in incomes and prices caused by a general trade depression. But if they adopt this method, and if at the same time they share a common International Currency with countries with more rigid economies, they may impose an intolerable deflationary strain upon these other countries. We may conclude therefore that one necessary condition for the efficient working of an International Currency is that there should be some International Monetary Authority endowed with sufficient powers to prevent a general trade depression from developing and from leading to a general deflation of prices and incomes in the various Member States.

In order to exercise such a control over trade depressions the International Monetary Authority must have the ultimate power of controlling the total supply of money within the Member States. This power it will possess if the International Currency, as suggested above, takes the form of the issue of notes by an International Bank under the control of the International Monetary Authority. When a general trade depression threatens to spread among the Member States, the International Bank should expand the issue of International Currency. This it could do, for example, by lending additional sums to the Central Banks of the various Member States, so that the monetary reserves of these banks were automatically increased. Alternatively the International Bank could issue new notes and invest them in appropriate securities on the stock exchanges of the various Member States. Such action would also increase the monetary reserves of the various national banking systems, since the persons from whom the securities were purchased would probably deposit a large part of the additional currency with the banks. The International Bank could thus increase the total currency throughout the Member States when there was a threat of a general depression in money expenditure and so in prices and incomes. It could, conversely, restrict the total supply of currency if a widespread inflationary movement of money prices and incomes threatened to develop among the Member States.

It is, however, uncertain how far this control over supplies of currency would alone suffice to prevent the development of trade booms and slumps. In the first place, when the monetary reserves of the national Central Banks were expanded as a result of the issue of additional supplies of International Currency, certain of these national banks might sterilize their supplies and prevent them from forming the base for a monetary expansion within their national territories. Such action would weaken and delay the monetary control of the International Bank. But, secondly, even if the International Bank obtained effective control over the total monetary supplies within the aggregate of Member States, it is not certain that these powers would be sufficient to ensure the prevention of a general trade depression. A general decline in monetary expenditure can be offset by an increase in monetary supplies only if someone is willing to borrow and spend the additional funds which are made available.

If business enterprise has become depressed by the prospect of a downward movement of prices and profits, the mere existence of plentiful monetary supplies available to be borrowed at low interest rates will not stimulate additional expenditure. In such circumstances the new funds may lie idle unless the public authorities themselves take steps to borrow additional sums to spend on public development, until private enterprise again becomes active. In other words, if the International Authority is to be able effectively to counteract general trade depressions, it may need to plan and control a significant part of the total public expenditure throughout the Member States. It is clear, however, that this would involve a wide extension of the economic powers and activities of the International Authority.

If sufficient economic powers of this kind were granted to the International Authority, a unified anti-depression policy would be possible. But even though general trade depressions were overcome in this way, many other causes of disequilibrium in the balances of payments between the Member States would remain. Let us suppose, for example, that state A produces coal, that state B produces oil, and that a technical change in industry leads, over a period of years, to the substitution of oil for coal as a source of power. In consequence B's demand for A's coal will fall, A's demand for B's oil will rise, and A will experience an excess of payments for imports, which she must finance by sending to B part of her reserves of the International Currency. Again, if A may neither impose a tariff on imports from B nor depreciate her currency in terms of B's currency, the necessary stimulation of A's exports and restriction of her imports can be obtained only by means of a monetary deflation of incomes and prices in A or a monetary inflation of prices and incomes in B.

In a dynamic world such readjustments will be necessary from time to time for various reasons, of which the above example provides only one particular illustration. The necessary deflation of prices in a state which is losing monetary reserves will lead to a reduction of profit margins and so to unemployment, unless money wage-rates are flexible and can be readily lowered in correspondence with the fall in prices. For this reason we may conclude that in order to ensure the efficient operation of an International Currency, considerable flexibility of money wage-rates and other costs must exist, even though the severe deflationary pressure of widespread trade depressions can be avoided. At all costs the individual states must be willing to give up the national planning of their internal prices and costs. If this fundamental condition cannot be satisfied, the necessary readjustments between the nations must be made by variations in the rate of exchange between their currencies.

There are certain further conditions which would ease the operation of an International Currency. In the first place, the very existence of free trade will ease any necessary readjustment of the balances of international payments. Suppose, for example, that a deflation of prices becomes necessary in a particular state in order to stimulate its exports to counterbalance an existing excess of imports. In such a case the absence of tariffs and, in particular, of quantitative quotas restricting the import of its products into other states will increase the ease with which it can expand its exports. This will reduce the extent to which the price deflation in the state concerned must proceed in order to stimulate its exports by the amount required. We may conclude therefore that a general lowering of restrictions on international trade will itself

54

contribute to the successful operation of a single International Currency.[1]

A second condition which is calculated to ease adjustments of this kind is greater freedom of international migration of labour. A deflation of prices and incomes in state A and an inflation of prices and incomes in state B, which becomes necessary to remove an excess of A's payments for imports, will lead to a reduction in the demand for labour in A and an increase in the demand for labour in B. The necessary adjustment will be eased if unemployed labour in A is free to move to meet the increased demand for labour in B.[2]

We may summarize by saying that an International Organization may be successfully built upon the economic bases of a common currency and of free international trade if various conditions are fulfilled. (1) The International Authority

[1] This conclusion may seem to contradict the argument expressed above that an appropriate change in its import restrictions is one possible method of readjusting a disequilibrium in the balance of any particular nation's international payments, and that for this reason the existence of free trade restricts the choice of methods of restoring equilibrium in the balance of payments between the nations. The contradiction is not, however, a real one. Appropriate variations in the relative levels of tariffs in different nations is one possible method of adjusting the balance of payments between them; but at the same time the lower is the general level of barriers to international trade, the more effective will be the other methods of adjusting the balance of international payments.

[2] In Chapter VIII other aspects of the regulation of international migration of labour will be discussed.

must have extensive powers over the total supply of money and over total public expenditure in order to overcome general trade depressions. (2) The individual Member States must renounce any intention of planning their own internal price levels and costs. (3) Wage-rates and other costs must possess a considerable flexibility within each Member State. (4) The successful operation of the system will be aided by the absence of hindrances to international trade and migration. In fact, an International Currency system is appropriate for a group of liberal economies which practise an internal policy of *laissez-faire*. It would also be appropriate to an International Authority which had extensive powers of planning and regulating economic and financial policy throughout the territories of the Member States. But it is not appropriate for an International Organization of states with divergent internal economic structures and policies, if those states desire to preserve a large measure of control over their own economic affairs.

Chapter IV

VARIABLE FOREIGN EXCHANGE RATES

IF the conditions enumerated at the end of the last chapter are not satisfied, it will not be possible successfully to operate an International Currency system and some other mechanism for adjusting the balance of payments between the various states must be found. It has already been suggested that, theoretically at least, two such methods exist. If a particular country has an excess of payments to make over its monetary receipts from other countries, it might reduce the payments to be made for imported goods by raising additional barriers on its import trade. Alternatively, it could make the necessary re-adjustment by depreciating the exchange value of its own currency in terms of the currencies of other countries. In this case, since more of its own currency would be needed to purchase a unit of foreign currency, the prices of imported foreign goods would rise in its home market; and at the same time, since less foreign money would be required to purchase a unit of its own currency, the prices of its exported goods would be reduced in foreign markets. For these reasons it would purchase less imported goods, but foreign purchasers would buy more of its exports; and in this way the excess of its international payments over its monetary receipts from other countries would disappear.

In the next chapter reasons will be given for believing that it is important to maintain trading conditions which are as free as possible between the Member States. In order to avoid the continual raising of trade barriers for the purpose of adjusting the balances of international payments between the various states, it would be preferable to rely upon the monetary mechanism of variable foreign exchange rates for this purpose. But it is important to realize that the abandonment of an International Currency system does not mean the abandonment of international monetary co-operation or of regulation of international monetary relations by an International Authority. In fact a system of variable exchange rates between the national currencies has serious disadvantages; and it will be the object of the International Authority to avoid or to mitigate these by means of its monetary regulations without, at the same time, preventing fluctuations in exchange rates which are necessary for the maintenance of equilibrium in the balance of payments of the various states.

The first and unavoidable disadvantage of abandoning an International Currency for a system of variable foreign exchange rates is the sacrifice of the convenience that would result from having the same unit of monetary account in all the Member States.

A second disadvantage of variable exchange rates is the added uncertainty which it involves for the traders of imported and exported goods in the various states. The possibility that the rate of exchange between two currencies may be varied in the course of an international transaction presents an additional obstacle to international trade. Methods for reducing this uncertainty will be discussed in a later section of this chapter.

Thirdly, the possibility of variations in the exchange rate between the various national currencies encourages the speculative movement of short-term capital from one currency to another in the anticipation of a fall in the exchange value of any particular currency. Such speculative capital movements play no useful economic role; and they may seriously complicate the problem of maintaining an equilibrium in the balances of international payments of the various nations. Various measures for mitigating this disadvantage will be discussed later in this chapter.

But the most serious danger of variable exchange rates remains still to be examined. It may be summed up in the phrase "competitive exchange depreciation." If one nation is faced with an unemployment problem, there are certain methods by which it can attempt to increase the markets for its products at the expense of other nations. It may, for example, impose restrictions on imports and may subsidize its exports in order to expand the internal and external markets for its own products at the cost of the producers in other nations. This will lead to an excess of receipts from exports over payments for imports on the part of the nation which adopts this policy, and this excess of receipts will be financed by means of a drain of gold or of other monetary balances from the other nations. So long as this situation is not disturbed by retaliatory action on the part of the other nations, the nation in question can undoubtedly expand the markets for its products.

This type of "beggar-my-neighbour" expansion can also be achieved by means of an unjustifiable depreciation of the foreign exchange value of a nation's currency. Let us assume that the balance of international payments and receipts of a particular nation are in equilibrium, but that at the same time it suffers from serious unemployment. This nation may take positive steps to depreciate the exchange value of its currency, even though there is no existing strain on its balance of international payments. If, for example, it is on the gold standard, it might deliberately devalue the gold value of its currency. Or, if it were not on the gold standard, its monetary authorities might deliberately use certain funds of its own currency—for example, the resources of an Exchange Equalization Fund—for the purchase of gold or of monetary balances in other countries. These additional purchases of foreign currency would lead to a depreciation in the exchange value of its currency. Such an exchange depreciation would restrict its internal demand for foreign goods by making foreign goods more expensive, and would expand the external demand for its own goods by reducing the price of its products in terms of foreign currencies. If at the same time it did nothing to stimulate its own internal demand for goods and services, it would succeed simply in expanding its markets at the expense of the markets of other nations, and in developing an excess of its monetary receipts over its monetary payments, which would drain money from other nations. The other nations would be likely to retaliate, and a series of competitive exchange depreciations might ensue.

For these reasons, even if variations in exchange rates are permitted as a means of adjusting the economic relations between the various nations, nevertheless, it is desirable to eliminate the possibility of unjustifiable exchange depreciations. The distinction between a "justifiable" and an "unjustifiable" exchange depreciation is to be found simply by reference to the balance of international payments of the nation whose exchange rate is to be depreciated. For example, suppose again that the balance of international payments of a particular nation is in equilibrium, but that it is suffering from a serious unemployment problem. If it adopts an internal policy of monetary expansion, it may increase the demand for its own products and so diminish unemployment; but this policy will also increase its demand for imports, and will lead to an excess of payments to other nations over receipts from other nations. To offset this disequilibrium in its balance of payments, the nation in question should be permitted to depreciate the exchange value of its currency to the necessary extent. But it should not be permitted to depreciate the exchange value of its currency in order to cure unemployment so long as its balance of payments remains in equilibrium; for this would merely impose a strain on other nations. On the other hand, if a country adopts an internal policy—(e.g. a policy of deflation of costs, prices and incomes)—which exerts a pressure upon other nations through a restriction of its national markets and a cheapening of its exports, it should be obliged to offset the resulting excess of its receipts from other nations by appreciating the exchange value of its currency.

In applying this criterion in practice various difficulties arise, because a nation's international payments and receipts include many items besides receipts from exports and payments for imports— such as receipts and payments for shipping services, for tourist traffic, for financial services, for payments of interest and dividends, for the granting of loans, the repayment of loans and various other capital transactions. A nation must be permitted to depreciate the exchange value of its currency when its international payments on all normal accounts are in excess of its receipts on all such accounts, and not simply when the value of its commodity imports exceeds the value of its commodity exports.

Owing to delays and difficulties in obtaining adequate statistics it is impossible to rely upon direct information about all the various items in each country's balance of payments, in order to judge when an exchange variation has become necessary. There is, however, a satisfactory short cut. If any particular country is subjected for a considerable time to any appreciable excess of payments to other countries on its international payments, the monetary authorities in that country will lose reserves of gold or of balances of foreign money to finance the excess of its payments. For this reason the following simple criterion may be used :—a country should depreciate the exchange value of its currency if it is persistently losing monetary reserves to other countries, and it should appreciate its currency if it is persistently receiving monetary reserves at the expense of other countries.

It may simplify this analysis to outline one possible mechanism by means of which these principles could be applied. Some "international means of payment" should be chosen, such as gold or the notes of an International Bank. The

Central Banks or other national monetary authorities would be required to fix the values of their national currencies by being obliged to buy and sell this "international means of payment" at a fixed price in terms of their own currencies. But the rates at which the various national currencies were pegged in this way to the "international means of payment" would be revised from time to time by an International Monetary Authority; and this body would have the power to compel any national Central Bank to depreciate the value of its currency in terms of the "international means of payment" if the Central Bank in question were persistently losing monetary reserves, and to appreciate its currency in the reverse conditions.

This process would operate by the method of trial and error. It might be impossible for the International Monetary Authority to judge accurately the precise degree to which a particular currency should be depreciated at any one time to remove a particular loss of monetary reserves. But the criterion suggested above will show the direction, if not the degree, in which the value of a currency should be changed; and by successive variations the International Monetary Authority can hope always to move the relative values of the various currencies more nearly towards their equilibrium levels. With this mechanism no country would be prevented from adopting an internal policy of monetary expansion by the fear that this would exert an impossible strain on its balance of payments; for in that case it would be permitted to depreciate the exchange value of its currency. On the other hand no country would be permitted by its national policy to put a strain on other countries: for as soon as it did so, the exchange value of its currency would be appreciated.

If gold were chosen as the "international means of payment" to which the national currencies should be provisionally pegged, the suggested system would correspond to the reintroduction of the gold standard—with the important proviso that the gold values of the various currencies would be revised from time to time in order to keep the balances of international payments in equilibrium. But if the national Central Banks held their monetary reserves in the form of notes issued by an International Bank or in the form of deposits held with such a Bank and if these notes or deposits formed the "international means of payments" for the provisional pegging of national currencies, a wider prospect of international economic co-operation would be opened up.

The International Monetary Authority would in this case be able to regulate the total supply of monetary reserves for the various Central Banks through its control of the note issue of the International Bank. The methods by which this could be done have already been described in the last chapter. If this system were adopted the International Monetary Authority might help to stabilize economic conditions by restricting the total supply of International Bank money in time of a world-wide boom and by increasing the total supply of such money in time of a widespread slump, even though the economic readjustments between the various nations were made by means of variations in the exchange values of their national currencies.

Moreover, the International Bank notes might in certain circumstances be also used for other purposes in addition to forming the medium for the monetary reserves of the national Central Banks. For example, in an International Organization of a number of Member States with divergent economic systems there might be some which adopted an internal and external policy of economic *laissez-faire*. In the case of such states the conditions which were noted in the last chapter for the successful operation of a fully developed International Currency might be satisfied. These states would be free to adhere to the full International Currency system described in the last chapter by adopting the notes of the International Bank as their own internal legal tender. At the same time, the remaining Member States which desired to retain greater powers of national economic planning would use the International Bank notes merely as the peg to which their national currencies should be fixed from time to time on the principles outlined in this chapter. There is no reason why such a dual system should not be made to work smoothly and efficiently.

But even in the case of the countries which do not adopt the International Bank notes for internal currency purposes, a more extended use of such notes might be made for international payments. For example, even though distinct national currencies remained legal tender for all payments, debts and contracts with the Member States, it might be permissible for international transactions between the citizens of these states to be expressed in terms of the International Bank notes. This arrangement might help to mitigate the uncertainties for international trade which arise from the possibility of variations in the rate of exchange between national currencies. Let us suppose that an importer in one state owes a certain sum of money to an exporter in another state. If this sum is fixed in terms of the creditor's currency, then the debtor runs a double exchange risk—first, that his currency may depreciate, and secondly, that the creditor's currency may appreciate before the debt is paid. But if the debt is fixed in terms of International Bank notes, the risk is shared. The debtor runs the risk that his currency may depreciate before he has purchased the necessary International Bank notes, and the creditor runs the risk that his currency may appreciate before he has sold the International Bank notes. But each party should know better than the other what is likely to be the future value of the currency of his own country; and since, by this arrangement, each party will bear the risk which attaches to the currency with which he is most familiar, the total risk will be diminished.

The International Bank might further diminish the uncertainties arising from the possibility of variations in exchange rates by organizing a market in the forward exchanges of the various currencies.[1] The Bank could offer to buy and to sell the various currencies for delivery at specified dates in the future at prices to be fixed now. In so far as it was able to balance a forward sale of dollars (e.g. to an English importer who had a debt to meet in the future in the United States) against a forward purchaser of dollars (e.g. from an American importer who had a future debt to meet in the United Kingdom), all exchange risks would be avoided. The English and the American importers would both know exactly the rates at which they would obtain the needed currencies in the future; and the International Bank would bear no risks, since its operations would offset each other. But in so far as the International Bank

---

[1] One currency, e.g. dollars, is said to be exchanged forward for another currency, e.g. pounds, if an exchange of dollars for pounds is arranged to take place at some date in the future at a rate of exchange which is fixed now.

undertook the forward sale of a particular currency which it could not itself cover by a forward purchase of the same currency, it would need either to bear the exchange risk itself or else to purchase immediately at the current price the currency which it had promised to sell forward.[1] If a reasonable premium were charged to cover possible risks, the International Bank should not lose upon this business—particularly if it represented the International Monetary Authority which alone had the power of altering exchange rates between the currencies of the Member States! The International Bank should, however, restrict these facilities to the finance of international trade or of other legitimate international transactions. For a forward exchange market can easily be misused for the purposes of exchange speculation; a person who is speculating on the depreciation of a particular currency may sell that currency forward—even though he possesses none of it—in the expectation that when the time comes he will be able to purchase it at a lower price.

Finally, the International Bank might take appropriate action to mitigate the evil effects of speculative movements of short-term capital

---

[1] The rather complicated way in which the relation between the "forward" and "spot" rates of exchange between two currencies normally depends upon the rate of interest in the two states cannot be explained here. The reader is referred to J. M. Keynes, *A Tract on Monetary Reform*, Chapter iii, or to Paul Einzig, *The Theory of Forward Exchange*, Part IV.

from one currency to another, movements which, as has been seen, are likely to be encouraged by the possibility of variations in the rates of exchange between the various currencies. National action for this purpose has usually taken one of two forms. In some cases such capital movements have been prevented by the imposition of complete state control over all dealings in foreign exchanges; and the extent to which Member States of an International Organization should be permitted to use this method is examined in Chapters VI and VII. An alternative method has been not to prevent such speculative movements, but to offset them by means of an Exchange Equalization Fund. For this purpose the national monetary authority holds a special fund of money, some invested in its own currency and some invested in gold or in the currencies of other countries. When, for example, speculators sell the currency of the home country for that of a particular foreign country, a transfer of part of the funds of the Exchange Equalization Fund from the currency of the foreign country to that of the home country is made in order to offset the speculative transfer.

National Exchange Equalization Funds are open to misuse. They may, for example, be used to engineer a competitive depreciation of a country's currency; for the authorities in charge of the fund might persist in purchasing additional balances of foreign currencies even though there were no speculative movement in the opposite direction to be offset. Such national funds might still be misused in a similar way even if the International Monetary Authority alone had the right of determining when the existing rates of exchange could be varied. For by a similar employment of its Exchange Equalization Fund a national monetary authority might place a strain on its own balance of payments and cause a loss in its published monetary reserves, with the object of inducing the International Monetary Authority to rule that the exchange value of its currency should be depreciated.

If the use of national Exchange Equalization Funds were forbidden to the Member States, the International Bank could itself fulfil the functions of an International Exchange Equalization Fund. The assets of the International Bank would presumably take the form either of money balances, or of loans and advances, or of securities, expressed in the currencies of the various Member States. A speculative movement of funds from currency A to currency B would be offset by the International Bank simply by transferring some of its assets from currency B to currency A. In this way the determination of exchange rates and the offsetting of speculative capital movements would be placed in the hands of the same authority.

*　　　*　　　*　　　*

71

The above paragraphs have been written with the object of outlining a system which would allow the individual states as free a hand as possible in the determination of their own national economic policies without allowing these policies to be developed at the expense of other states. If a system of this kind were adopted, it would not of course exclude voluntary international economic co-operation for special purposes between a more limited number of Member States. To take an example, with the system outlined in this chapter, the prosecution of an anti-slump policy would be primarily in the hands of the Member States rather than in those of the International Authority. But this would not preclude co-operation between a number of like-minded states in the development of their anti-slump policies. It is true that, with the system outlined above, any state would be free to attempt to meet a general trade depression by means of a policy of monetary expansion and of increased public expenditure; and it is also true that this state would be allowed to depreciate the exchange value of its currency if this was necessary to enable it to continue with this policy. Nevertheless, it is also true that such a state would find that this policy was easier to adopt and more efficient in its working if it were accompanied by a similar policy, similarly timed, in a number of other states. There would be nothing to prevent a number of Member States from setting up an

International Commission of their own to arrange for co-operative action in their national monetary policies and in the timing of their public expenditures, provided that their action did not offend against the limited number of restrictions imposed upon them by the scheme suggested in this chapter. All that is suggested is that effective and useful monetary co-operation need not be confined exclusively to states which are so like-minded.

c*

Chapter V

INTERNATIONAL TRADE

It is clear that one of the major concerns of an International Authority would be with the trade between the Member States. Indeed, the principles upon which international trade is conducted, taken together with the choice of an international monetary mechanism, constitute the core of the economic problems of an International Organization; and in this connection the most important point to decide is whether the principle of free trade between the Member States should be made a condition of membership of the International Organization.

The arguments for a free trade system are very powerful, although they have frequently been misunderstood and mis-stated by their advocates. Economic conditions differ for various reasons in different countries. Let us suppose that in country A a pair of shoes costs three times as much to produce as a sack of potatoes, whereas in state B a pair of shoes costs only twice as much to produce as a sack of potatoes. Then A can produce three more sacks of potatoes at the expense of producing one less pair of shoes, while B can produce one more pair of shoes at the expense of producing only two less sacks of potatoes. Thus if A concentrates on producing potatoes and B on producing shoes, the total production of potatoes will rise, without any decline in the total production of shoes. In other words if each country specializes on the production of the commodities in which it has the greatest advantages of productivity (or the smallest · disadvantages of productivity) in comparison with other countries, the total world production of commodities will be increased; and provided that the commodities in question are capable of being transported and traded from country to country, the standard of living will thus be raised in all countries.

If competitive conditions prevail in the countries concerned, freedom of international trade will bring about the desired specialization of production between the various countries. To revert to the example given above, so long as a pair of shoes can be produced in state B at the cost of only two sacks of potatoes but is worth as much as three sacks of potatoes in state A, it will pay traders to export shoes from B to A and potatoes from A to B. This trade will bring about the required specialization of A upon potato production and of B upon shoe production.[1]

[1] This does not necessarily imply that *no* potatoes will be produced in B and *no* shoes in A. If there are some districts in B which are peculiarly fertile for potato cultivation and some shoe factories in A which have a specially high productivity, the working of the competitive prices will not, of course, eliminate them.

This is the simple classical argument for free trade. Its fundamental validity is clear, and there is little doubt that for this reason a free trade policy should be taken as the basis of the commercial policy for the International Organization. Any restrictions on international trade which were allowed to remain would require special justification. It remains, therefore, to be seen what special arguments may be advanced for the imposition of trade barriers. In addition it will be necessary to enquire to what extent a free trade policy can be applied—or indeed can be said to have any meaning—in the case of a "planned" economy in which foreign trade is a state monopoly.

The first serious argument for a national policy of protection is that it may be used as a means of reducing unemployment. Certain aspects of the relation between trade protection and unemployment have been examined incidentally in the two previous chapters. Thus a particular country which is suffering from a serious problem of general unemployment may impose a tariff in order to expand its own industrial activity at the expense of goods imported from abroad. If at the same time it does nothing to expand the total volume of purchasing power of its inhabitants, it can at the best succeed in expanding its own markets at the expense of other countries; and it can do this only if other countries do not retaliate. Clearly this case presents no valid argument for the sacrifice of a free trade policy.

But a country which is suffering from a serious problem of unemployment may adopt an internal policy of monetary expansion at the same time that it raises additional barriers on imports. In this case the expansion of its own internal markets will not necessarily be at the expense of other countries; the additional trade restrictions may simply prevent a rise in its imports which would otherwise have resulted from the expansion of the purchasing power of its inhabitants. It has already been argued in the two previous chapters that protective measures of this kind may enable a country to undertake an internal policy of reflation without putting a strain on its balance of international payments and without depreciating the exchange value of its currency. But if a monetary organization of the kind outlined in the previous chapter is adopted, any necessary readjustments of the balance of payments will be obtained by appropriate changes in exchange rates; and this will remove any need for import restrictions as a method of maintaining equilibrium in the balances of international payments of the Member States.

There is, however, a more substantial argument in favour of a protective policy as a means of preventing unemployment. A distinction must be drawn between two types of unemployment, which may be called "general" and "special" unemployment. "General" unemployment may be said to exist during a trade depression when there is a general superfluity of labour in the economic system, i.e. when the demand for additional labour in any industries which may still be expanding is less than sufficient to balance the surplus of labour in the depressed occupations. But in the absence of such "general" unemployment, "special" unemployment may exist in particular industries or occupations or districts as a result of special causes. One example will be sufficient to illustrate this distinction. A change in industrial technique may lead to an abrupt decline in the demand for coal, as a result of the use of new fuels. This decline in the demand for coal will cause unemployment among coal miners, even though there may be a scarcity of labour in many other expanding occupations. For it is not possible for a coal miner to move at once to another occupation situated in another district and requiring another skill and training. For such reasons "special" unemployment may persist for a considerable time as a result of any far-reaching change in economic structure.

The previous arguments of this chapter have been limited to showing that a policy of protection is neither a necessary nor a suitable policy for the cure of "general" unemployment. They do not prove that such a policy is inappropriate as a means for mitigating "special" unemployment. The reduction of an existing tariff may itself constitute just such a structural economic change as to cause a serious problem of "special" unemployment. If, for example, agricultural activity has been enabled to persist in a particular country behind the shelter of a highly protective tariff, the removal of this tariff is likely to cause unemployment and distress among agriculturalists for a considerable time, even though there are other expanding occupations into which they can eventually be drawn. Since the institution of an International Organization on the basis of a free trade policy would immediately involve the removal of many trade barriers, it is important to examine in rather more detail the effects both upon "general" and upon "special" unemployment of such an economic upheaval.

If all the Member States reduce their trade barriers *pari passu* this should not cause any problems of "general" unemployment in any one of them. For just as quickly as the reduction of tariffs by any particular country opens part of its internal market to the competition of additional foreign imports, its external markets will be expanded by the reduction of tariffs in other countries. The total demand for its goods will not be reduced; but, nevertheless, for a considerable time it may suffer from a problem of "special" unemployment as workers are being transferred from the industries which are contracting as a result of more intense foreign competition on the home market, to the industries which are expanding as a result of the easier access to foreign markets for its exports.

But one Member State may previously have practised a much more protective commercial policy than other Member States. In this case a general abolition of trade barriers would mean that this particular state must reduce such barriers much more extensively than other states. It might, therefore, appear at first sight that this country would suffer from "general" unemployment, because the invasion of its internal market by foreign goods would be less than compensated by the extension of its foreign market. In order to see how the two problems of "general" and "special" unemployment might be met in such a case, let us examine an extreme case. Let us suppose that there has been heavy agricultural protection in a particular industrialized country, and that this country alone removes its agricultural tariffs and quotas without any simultaneous reduction of trade barriers in other countries.

The first result will be a fall in the demand for home-produced agricultural products in the country in question, as a result of the free import of the cheaper foreign produce. This will reduce the cost of living and so raise the standard of living for the non-agricultural workers in the country. But it will cause a reduction of production, employment and incomes in the previously protected agricultural occupations without any immediate counterbalancing extension of the demand for other home-produced products. The country would appear to be suffering from "general" as well as from "special" unemployment. By what mechanism can the total demand for goods and services be so raised as to counterbalance the reduction in the demand for home-produced agricultural products?

The removal of the protection to home agriculture will have given rise to an excess of payments to other countries in the balance of international payments of the country in question; for its agricultural imports will have risen without any immediate rise in its receipts from exports. If the monetary mechanism suggested in the last chapter is adopted, this position should be readjusted by an exchange depreciation of the country's currency. This exchange depreciation, by raising the prices of all foreign goods in the home market, will give some measure of protection to all the home industries and occupations —including agriculture. The exchange depreciation will at the same time cheapen the price in foreign currencies of the country's manufactures and other products, and this will give, as it were, a subsidy to all the country's exports. This measure of protection of home markets and subsidization of external markets which results from exchange depreciation will have a double effect: it will restore the country's balance of international payments, and it will increase the total demand for the country's goods and services as an offset to the decline in the demand for its agricultural products.

If for any particular reason an exchange depreciation which is sufficient to restore equilibrium to the country's balance of international payments should prove insufficient to remove the whole of the country's "general" unemployment problem, a policy of internal economic expansion may be adopted. For example, the monetary authorities may extend new loans and provide new funds at reduced rates of interest; and, if necessary, the public authorities may borrow some of these new funds to spend on additional schemes of public construction. The consequent demand of private or public enterprise for capital goods will help to cure the problem of "general" unemployment; and this increase in economic activity will in turn stimulate the demand for other goods and services. As a result of this internal expansion, the demand for imports will probably be still further raised; and for this reason some additional measure of exchange depreciation may become necessary to restore the country's balance of international payments. This would provide a further measure of protection of home industries and of subsidization of exports, which would help to cure the remaining problem of "general" unemployment.

It is clear, then, that any "general" unemployment resulting from tariff reductions may be cured by an appropriate policy of exchange depreciation—as outlined in the previous chapter —combined, if necessary, with internal monetary and economic expansion. But the resultant "special" unemployment could not be cured by these means. To continue the previous example, "special" unemployment would persist among the farmers and agricultural workers who had just lost their protection, until a considerable number of them or of their children had been able to become engineers or builders—if we may select machinery to represent the exports which are stimulated by the exchange depreciation and the construction of houses to represent the internal activities stimulated by the policy of monetary and economic expansion.

Such transitions are, however, often slow and may be accompanied by great hardship and suffering. The hand-loom weavers of England whose jobs were destroyed by the invention of mechanical weaving, and the coal miners of South Wales after the great reduction in British exports of coal are striking examples of the special unemployment and distress caused by serious changes of economic structure. Special measures of two types may be taken to mitigate this problem. Payments in relief of distress may be granted by the state or by other public authorities in such cases. Steps may also be taken by the state to speed up and to ease the transition itself. For example, the particular workers concerned may be given special facilities for retraining for new occupations, the costs of removal of them and their families to new districts may be met in whole or in part by the state, official bodies may be instituted to find suitable work for them, and new industries may be encouraged by subsidy or otherwise to settle in the specially distressed districts.

But even if widespread national measures of this kind were taken in the Member States to ease the transition, the sudden and complete elimination of all trade barriers by the International Organization would undoubtedly give rise to serious problems of "special" unemployment. For this reason the constitution of the International Organization should probably not demand the immediate removal of all trade barriers. But the reductions of such barriers should be effected over a series of years; they should be speeded up in years of expanding business activity, and postponed whenever there was a widespread threat of general depression and unemployment. Such a gradual approach to free trade, combined with national measures of relief for special distress and of transference of workers to new occupations, would probably prove workable: the sudden introduction of free trade without adequate national measures of relief or of labour transference might well condemn the International Organization to collapse and failure.

This argument constitutes a serious reason for a gradual approach to free trade; but it does not justify a rejection of the free trade principle as the ultimate basis for the commercial policy of the Member States, to which they should be obliged to approach as quickly as is possible. The permanent protection of an occupation to prevent "special" unemployment would involve the permanent sacrifice of a possible all-round rise in the standard of living in order to avoid the temporary difficulties of transition. If, for example, the hand-loom weavers had in some way or another been permanently protected from the competition of mechanical looms, we should still to-day be clothed at great toil and expense by such handwork. The temporary transition must, no doubt, be eased, and the particular workers who, for no fault of their own, are suddenly threatened with unemployment and poverty, must receive special assistance. But the change itself must not be prevented.

We may turn now to certain arguments of a different character in favour of a protective policy. It is possible in certain circumstances that a particular country by imposing a tariff may gain at the expense of other countries by improving the terms on which it conducts its trade with the other countries. Thus, if a particular country reduces its expenditure on foreign goods by imposing a tariff on imports, the immediate effect will probably be the development of an excess of its receipts from other countries over its payments to other countries. To readjust its balance of payments there may need to be an appreciation of the exchange value of its currency, which will raise the price of its exports in terms of the currencies of the other countries and will thus restrict its exports to correspond with the fall in its imports. Alternatively, if the country in question is tied to an international monetary standard, the reduction in its demand for imports will lead to a drain of monetary reserves from other countries; and this drain can be stopped only by a rise of prices in the country imposing the tariff or by a decline of prices in the other countries. But whether the balance of international payments be readjusted by an exchange rate variation or by an adjustment of internal prices, the price in foreign currencies of the exports of the country imposing the tariff will rise in relation to the price at which it can obtain its imports in foreign markets. It will, in fact, be trading on better terms at the expense of the countries from which it is purchasing.

This will not in all circumstances bring a gain to the country which is imposing the tariff. If— as is probable—the other countries retaliate by the imposition of a tariff, this is likely to shift the terms of trade back again by the reverse monetary mechanism to the disadvantage of the country which was the first to raise a tariff. In this case there may in the end be no substantial net change in the terms of trade for any of the various countries; but they will all lose through the consequent loss in the international specialization of production. It follows also from this argument that if all the Member States of an International Organization reduce their tariffs *pari passu*, no one of them is likely to lose substantially by a change in the terms of trade to its disadvantage; for just as quickly as it increases its demand for foreign goods by lowering its tariff, so the foreign demand for its goods will rise by the lowering of tariffs elsewhere. On the other hand all the states will gain by the increase in the total volume of international trade.

But even if a country is able to shift the terms of trade in its favour by imposing a tariff without meeting with the retaliation of other countries, it will not necessarily gain. It is probable that a single country will not be able to move the terms of trade very substantially in its favour; and it may well find that it has obtained only a small advantage in the terms of its trade at the cost of a considerable diminution in the total volume of its trade. In such a case the loss in the total volume of its trade may more than counterbalance the fact that it is making a slightly larger gain on the trade which remains to it. There are, nevertheless, circumstances in which a country can gain at the expense of others by imposing a tariff. For example, a particular country may be the most important purchaser in the world market for some product; and it is possible at the same time that the foreign producers of this product find it difficult either to expand the alternative markets for the product or to shift over to the production of other commodities. In such a case the buying country may be in a position very considerably to reduce the price at which it can obtain its imports through a moderate reduction of its purchases. It may in fact be able to reap a large gain at the expense of the producing countries.

This possibility should not, however, modify the adoption of the principle of free trade for the commercial relations between the Member States of an International Organization. For any national gain of this kind is obtained solely at the expense of some other country. The imposition of a tariff nearly always benefits some one class of persons. The producers in a protected industry are in a better position to obtain high profits or high wages for themselves; but the existence of such a vested interest within any nation—however vocal it may be—does not justify the maintenance of a tariff which is to the disadvantage of the national community as a whole. In the same way the maintenance of a particular tariff may in certain circumstances benefit the inhabitants of the protected nation; but this cannot justify the maintenance of a national tariff, which is detrimental to the interests of the international community of nations.

It is sometimes argued that the payment of low wages in another country justifies the imposition of a tariff in a country of high wages in order to protect that country's standard of living. This argument is based upon a misunderstanding of the basis upon which the advantages of international trade are to be obtained. Let us suppose that country A by paying low wages is able to undercut the prices of certain products of country B. Can B gain by imposing a tariff on imports from A? Certainly the producers of the protected commodities in B will gain from the tariff; but this is true of any protective tariff imposed in any circumstances, and has nothing to do with the payment of specially low wages in A. The proper question is whether the whole community in B can gain from the imposition of the tariff. It is possible that if the competition from A has developed quickly a temporary tariff in B might be justifiable on the grounds of the "special" unemployment that would otherwise appear. But this argument again has nothing to do with the payment of low wages in A; for it refers equally to any abrupt change in the conditions of foreign trade. It may be that by imposing the tariff country B is able to obtain her imports from A on better terms than before. But this argument also has nothing to do with the low wages paid in A; for the ability to shift the terms of trade to the national advantage does not depend upon the level of wages in other countries. It is possible that as an immediate result of a reduction in the price of A's products, B's balance of international payments will be thrown out of equilibrium by her excessive purchases of goods from A, and that this will drain monetary reserves from B and will impose a monetary deflation on B. But in this case, if the monetary organization outlined in the previous chapter is adopted, the necessary readjustment can be brought about by an exchange depreciation of B's currency. The fundamental fact that must not be forgotten is that everyone in B, as a consumer, will gain from buying goods at a cheaper price from A. In fact B as a whole will gain if it can obtain more goods by using its available factors of production to produce exports to exchange for the cheap products of A than it can obtain by using these factors at home to produce the goods for itself; and it makes no difference to this argument whether the cheapness of the products in A is due to low wages or to high productivity or to any other peculiar set of conditions in A.

This does not imply that B may not lose economically from a cheapening in the cost of certain products in A. For if A and B compete for export markets in certain other countries, the cheapening of costs in A may shift the demand of these other countries from B's to A's products and may thus move the terms of trade to the disadvantage of B. But can B prevent this by imposing a tariff? Generally speaking she cannot raise tariffs against A's goods in the other markets in which A's competition is harming her; and as far as the protection of B's home market is concerned, there is nothing to add to the previous arguments. If, however, the markets in which A and B compete include certain territories which are B's colonies, then B will be able to gain by imposing a trade barrier in these colonies against A's goods. In this case B's gain will be at the expense both of A, who is excluded from competing in these closed colonial markets, and of the inhabitants of the colony, who are prevented from buying the cheaper products of A. Since gains of this type should presumably not be permitted, we may conclude that the "low wage" argument for protection does not present a valid reason for abandoning the principle of free trade for the International Organization.

Two further arguments for national protection, which we may call the "infant industry" and the "social" arguments, might retain some validity in the International Organization. It is often argued that in order to establish a new industry in a particular locality—or in order to promote general industrial activity in an agricultural community—a temporary measure of protection is necessary, but that as experience is gained and as costs are thereby reduced, the industry will become self-supporting without protection. Economists are generally in agreement that, in certain cases, a valid argument of this kind may exist for the temporary imposition of a tariff. Nevertheless it is doubtful whether this should be permitted to break the free trade rule for the nations constituting the International Organization. Temporary support to a new industry can be given by a direct subsidy from the national budget; and this method of granting special favours to a particular industry has the additional advantage of making the cost of the favours apparent to the whole community. If the individual Member States preserve the right of granting subsidies and bounties, the "infant industry" argument is no longer a valid reason for breaking the free trade rule.

A similar reasoning may be applied to the "social" argument for protection. In a number of industrialized countries, for example, agriculture has been protected partly in order to preserve a rural population for social reasons. In cases of this kind also direct subsidies may be paid to the particular branch of economic activity which for non-economic reasons it is desired to foster. They are as effective as a protective tariff, and have the added advantage of making clear the economic cost of the policy.[1]

[1] Military and strategic considerations—the desire to be more nearly self-supporting in foodstuffs or in other vital products in case of war—have often led to the protection of various industries. It is to be presumed that the political aspects of the International Organization would remove the necessity for such defensive considerations as between the Member States; but considerations of defence against states outside the International Organization might

We may summarize the argument up to this point by saying that valid arguments for some measure of national protection would exist in an International Organization on three grounds: to relieve "special" unemployment, to protect infant industries and to pursue certain social or other non-economic objectives. But provided that the transition to free trade is gradual and that the Member States retain the right of subsidizing directly particular industries and occupations, these arguments do not constitute a conclusive case for the abandonment of the free trade principle by the International Organization.

But we must now pass to the more complicated problem of the foreign trade of the "planned" economy. The previous arguments of this chapter can be applied directly only to the "liberal" economies; for the very term "free trade" implies an economic system in which individuals are permitted to compete with each other in undertaking trade transactions. In the completely "planned" economy free trade in this sense is an impossibility—for the simple reason that foreign trade is a government monopoly and individuals are not free to take part either in internal or in international trade. On what principles, then, should the International Authority regulate the

still necessitate the fostering of certain industries in certain of the Member States. This matter would clearly be in the province of the International Authority, which might, for example, pay subsidies to particular industries in particular localities directly from its own budget.

trading conditions of those of the Member States which have "planned" economies?

The fundamental point to realize is that a "planned" economy *can* obtain the same advantages from international trade as a "liberal" economy. It can use part of its available productive forces to produce goods for exchange for other goods on foreign markets whenever more of the products which it needs can be obtained in this way than by producing the goods for itself at home. It has already been explained at some length in Chapter II that a "planned" economy may, if it chooses, make use of a system of pricing and costing which will enable it to compare the internal costs of producing various products. If use is made of a costing system of this kind, the authorities in charge of the foreign trade of a "planned" economy can apply what may be called the free trade principle to their transactions. To achieve this object they should (*a*) export goods whenever the internal costs of producing and transporting these goods is lower than the price which can be obtained in foreign markets for them, and (*b*) import commodities for home use whenever the price at which they are priced at home is higher than the cost of purchasing and transporting the foreign produce.

The only question which would remain to be solved would be the exchange rate at which the national money of the "planned" economy should be valued for the purposes of making these calculations of relative prices and costs of home-produced and foreign goods. In a "planned" economy monetary transactions with foreign countries will presumably not be left to private individuals, so that there will be no free foreign exchange market in which competitive forces can determine an actual exchange rate. But, nevertheless, a rate of exchange for the purposes of the calculations of the authority in charge of the country's foreign trade could be determined on the principles outlined in the previous chapter. The monetary authorities could fix a rate of exchange for accounting purposes at a level which was considered suitable to equalize the country's monetary receipts from exports and other sources with its monetary payments for imports and other purposes. If at this rate of exchange the country's monetary payments exceeded its receipts, the exchange value of its money could be depreciated for accounting purposes. This would cause the authorities in charge of its foreign trade to increase exports and to diminish imports, so long as they acted in accordance with the pricing and costing principles outlined above. For, as in the case of "liberal" economies, the depreciation in the exchange value of the country's currency would raise the prices in its own currency at which it could purchase foreign goods and at which it could sell its exports in foreign markets.

In order to ensure that this free trade principle was applied as fully as possible, the International

Authority would need to appoint representatives to the national boards of control over the foreign trade of the Member States with "planned" economies; and these representatives would need to possess the final power of decision over the actions of such national bodies. Nothing less than this would give the International Authority a real power of regulation of the international trade of such Member States. Moreover the need for the application of a general formula based on relative prices and costs to determine international trade relations becomes greater as national controls over foreign trade become more frequent and more extensive. For a national monopoly of foreign trade is in a particularly strong position to use its monopolistic powers to obtain economic advantages at the expense of other states. By threatening to cancel its customary purchases from a particular country, a national import board may obtain a low price quotation at the expense of exploiting the producers in a foreign country. By threatening to withhold all sales to a particular market, a national export board may squeeze a monopoly price from the consumers in some other country. If a number of important countries have monopolized their foreign trade, there is a grave danger that the remaining "liberal" countries would be forced to monopolize their own foreign trade in order to retaliate, even though they wished to maintain a liberal system. International economic relations would degenerate quickly into the chaos of a perpetual economic war.

If, however, a simple formula is devised to regulate foreign trading relations—such as the formula suggested above that comparative prices and costs should determine trade channels on the free trade principle—and if an international control is instituted to ensure that this formula is observed, the foreign trade of "planned" economies could be conducted on orderly commercial principles. As long as a number of "liberal" economies remained, there would be a nucleus of competition in which world market prices for different commodities could be determined; and the comparison of internal costs and external prices could be made for the "planned" economies on the basis of these world market prices. If these free markets became too restricted those in charge of the foreign trade of each of the "planned" economies would be obliged to use the prices in the other "planned" economies as their basis of comparison.

A system of this kind presents the only alternative to an economic chaos. In principle it is simple; but its actual application would, no doubt, give rise to difficulties and complexities. In particular its application depends upon the existence of some system of internal pricing and costing inside the "planned" economies; for unless this exists, there is no basis upon which the comparison of internal prices and costs can be

D

made. The system could not in any case be applied without modifications. For, if the "liberal" economies are to be permitted the right to grant subsidies to particular industries or occupations in order to protect infant industries or to encourage an occupation for social reasons or to mitigate the problem of "special" unemployment, a similar freedom of action must be left to the "planned" economies. But in a planned economy there are so many ways of subsidizing a particular industry—whether by direct subsidy from the state budget or by not requiring it to make so high a profit as other industries or by providing raw materials or capital to it at specially low prices—that it is not possible to limit and define this right as clearly as in the case of the "liberal" economies. The authorities in a "planned" economy have very extensive powers of encouraging particular industries by these various kinds of subsidy, while a "liberal" economy would be confined to a direct subsidy from the budget. But any attempt to restrict the internal policy of the "planned" economies—however logical it may be—would probably prove impracticable, in the absence of a more or less complete control by the International Authority over the whole economic system of the "planned" economies.

Further, as its very name suggests, a "planned" economy might desire to plan ahead not only its internal economy but also its foreign trade.

Whereas in a "liberal" economy the forces of competitive markets give rise to daily changes in prices, output and employment, in the "planned" economy these quantities are determined for some time ahead and are then subjected to a change of plan from time to time as circumstances require. It might reasonably be the desire of a "planned" economy to determine ahead for a considerable period the quantities of its imports and its exports and to fix these by long-term contracts with foreign buyers and sellers. No objection could be taken to such action, even though it does for the time being remove the influence of changes in relative prices and costs upon imports and exports. All that is essential is that the "planned" foreign trade should be revised from time to time and that it should be revised upon the basis of a comparison of internal and external prices and costs in the way that has been suggested above.

In addition to the problem of the foreign trade of the completely "planned" economy, similar problems would arise on a smaller scale in the case of the Member States whose generally liberal economies were modified by certain elements of state control. These problems could be settled on the same lines. Thus national import and export boards set up to control particular markets could be regulated on the same principles by the International Authority. Moreover international cartels or monopolies might be submitted to the control of the International Authority in order to ensure that the products concerned were made available to all consumers throughout the Member States at a price equivalent to the cost of production and transport. In particular, the International Authority should supervise the operations of the various bodies which already control prices, production, sales or exports of various primary commodities such as tin, rubber and tea.[1]

[1] The principles upon which these bodies should be regulated are discussed in Chapter IX below.

Chapter VI

INTERNATIONAL CAPITAL MOVEMENTS

THE productivity of labour in any country, and thus the standard of living of that country, depends not only upon the quality and efficiency of the labour itself. It is also much affected by the natural resources in land and raw materials with which the country is endowed and by the capital instruments and the technical knowledge with which the workers are equipped. A high standard of living depends on the absence of any pressure of population upon the available natural resources, and on the possession of an abundant capital equipment and of advanced technical knowledge and training. In a later chapter the effects of international population movements upon the standard of living will be examined, while the present chapter is devoted to the problems of capital equipment and, incidentally, of technical knowledge.

There are a number of wealthy communities, such as the United States of America and the United Kingdom, where there is a relative abundance of capital equipment; and in these countries, while the output per head of the workers is high, the need for additional capital is comparatively small, with the consequence that the rate of interest which producers will offer for capital extensions is relatively low. On the other hand there are many undeveloped or comparatively poor countries in which there is a scarcity of capital in relation to the number of workers or to the available natural resources. These countries may be either in the position of India, Japan or China where there is a considerable pressure of population upon the available land and natural resources, or they may be in the position of some of the South American Republics where both population and capital are scarce. But in both cases the scarcity of capital in relation either to labour or to the available natural resources or to both will prevent the productivity of labour from rising as it otherwise might, and will lead to the levy of high interest charges for the little capital that does exist.

In normal conditions capital moves naturally from the wealthy to the undeveloped countries in search of higher yields. This movement, in so far as it develops, has two outstanding advantages. In the first place, it leads to an increase in total world production. For the investment of new machinery, for example, in an undeveloped area where capital is scarce and where the productivity of capital is therefore high will increase total production more than the investment of an equivalent amount of machinery in a country where the most productive uses for capital have already been satisfied.

Secondly, international capital movements from rich to poor countries are likely to reduce existing differences in the standard of living. Such movements should benefit both the lending and the borrowing countries. For the lending country should be able to obtain a somewhat higher rate of interest on capital lent abroad than on capital lent at home; and at the same time the borrowing country should be able to obtain capital at a somewhat lower rate of interest from abroad than from its internal resources. Since the rich and the poor countries would share the gain in this way, it is not at all certain that international inequalities of income would be reduced.

It is, however, probable that in many cases the income of the poor countries would be raised much more than that of the wealthy countries by a movement of capital from the latter to the former. For not only does the improved capital equipment of the poor and undeveloped territories directly increase the productivity of labour in these areas; it has also a number of indirect effects. In the first place, an initial rise in the standard of living resulting from an inflow of foreign capital may enable the inhabitants of the country in question to start saving and accumulating capital for themselves out of their higher incomes. An initial stimulus from abroad may thus help to start a more rapid industrial development financed from internal funds. Secondly, the borrowing of funds from abroad for the initiation of schemes of capital development in an undeveloped country will probably involve the services of foreign engineers, technicians and skilled workers to construct and, for a time, to work the new capital installations. Directly as a result of this and indirectly as a result of the greater familiarity with modern technique the inhabitants of the backward territory may themselves learn new skills and new methods of production. The gradual extension of such knowledge is in many cases the most important factor in raising productivity in backward areas, and so in equalizing international standards of living.

Borrowing of capital from abroad may in these ways be the initial stimulus for the "modernization" of backward areas; and great increases in productivity can be brought about by the use of modern methods of large-scale production both in industry and in certain agricultural occupations. The possibility of such revolutions in technical methods will be greatly increased if conditions of free trade can at the same time be guaranteed by the means suggested in the previous chapters; for in that case the backward areas will be free to develop the foreign markets for the goods which they can most easily produce on a large scale. In favourable circumstances wise foreign borrowing by an undeveloped country may directly and indirectly help to raise the standard of living out of all proportion to the sums actually borrowed.

The main obstacle which stands in the way of free movements of capital between the nations is the difficulty of transfer of the capital from the lending to the borrowing country and, later, of the payment of interest and sinking fund by the debtor to the creditor nation. A foreign loan involves an exchange of the lending country's currency into the money of the borrowing country in order to transfer the money loan to the borrowers. This will impose a strain upon the lending country's balance of international payments, unless the borrowing country actually buys from the lending country the capital goods which it needs. But if the borrowing country spends the proceeds of the loan in other countries, the lending country will need to expand its receipts from exports or to contract its payments for imports in order to offset its capital payment to the borrowing country. This it must do by one of the means discussed in Chapters III and IV —i.e. either by an internal deflation or by a depreciation of the exchange value of its currency; but in a world in which there are serious barriers imposed upon its exports to other markets, it may experience great difficulties in making the necessary adjustments to its balance of international payments. Many countries have in fact placed embargoes of one kind or another upon foreign lending in order to ease the strain on their balances of international payments which might result from such lending. In the United Kingdom, for example, an embargo has been placed since 1931 on the issue of foreign loans on the London capital market; and various countries which have instituted rigid systems of exchange control have used these controls to prevent all capital movements abroad.

The willingness of countries to lend abroad has also been much reduced in recent years by the history of defaults on numerous foreign investments since 1929. These defaults have been caused by many factors, one of the most important of which was the difficulty of transferring the sums for interest and repayment of capital from the debtor to the creditor countries. In order to prevent an intolerable burden upon their balances of payments the debtor countries must be able to develop an excess of exports to counterbalance their purchases of foreign currency for the service of their debts. If tariffs or other trade barriers are continually raised against such countries when their exports expand, their difficulties may become unbearable. Again it is clear that an efficient and adaptable machinery for adjusting the balance of payments between debtor and creditor countries is a *sine qua non* of free international capital movements.

A second important condition for the successful operation of international capital movements is that efficient measures should be taken to prevent the development of serious world-wide deflations. Many foreign investments are fixed in terms of money both as to the capital sum and as to the annual interest to be paid on the capital. A widespread and serious fall in commodity prices and so in money incomes greatly increases the real burden of debts which are fixed in money values, and for this reason the insecurity of foreign loans is greatly increased during a world-wide trade depression.

The importance of these factors may be illustrated by the experiences following the great depression which started in 1929. In the years immediately preceding 1929 the rich creditor countries—and in particular the United States of America—were lending considerable sums abroad both to undeveloped areas such as South American and also to Germany, whose heavy borrowings were enabling her to meet the reparations payments. The Americans were lending money to Germany and Germany was paying reparations to other countries, which in turn used these sums to pay war debts to the United States. The overseas debtor countries which concentrated on the production of foodstuffs and raw materials for export were enabled to meet the interest and sinking fund on their debts from the new loans which were being made to them and from the relatively high demand for their exports on the part of the prosperous industrialized countries.

The whole system was suddenly broken by the great depression. The rich creditor countries ceased to lend abroad as soon as the depression led to doubt about the solvency of their debtors, and in many cases attempted to withdraw the capital funds which they had already lent. This put a double strain upon the balances of payments of the debtor countries, which had to develop their exports or to restrict their imports to balance both the cessation of an annual inflow of new capital and also the actual withdrawals of capital. Two factors added to this problem. The fall in money prices, particularly in the prices of the foodstuffs and raw materials exported by many debtor countries, greatly increased the real surplus of goods which they had to sell to repay a given money debt. At the same time many of the principal creditor countries, and in particular the United States of America, raised additional trade restrictions on imports which made it still more difficult for the debtor countries to obtain an equilibrium in their balances of payments.

The stream of American loans to Germany and other countries had already been much reduced before the depression, as a result of the counter-attraction of stock exchange speculation in the United States in 1928 and 1929. In any case it could not have continued indefinitely; and some revision of reparations and war debt payments might in any case have become inevitable. But if the great depression had been avoided, there would have been no such sudden break in confidence and no such sudden cessation of foreign lending and abrupt recall of outstanding loans. There would have been no abrupt deflation of prices to raise the real burden of reparations, of war debts and of foreign indebtedness in general. If, in addition, there had been a reasonably reliable mechanism for the adjustment of the balances of international payments which had allowed the debtor countries to develop an export surplus with relative ease, the problem would have remained a manageable one.

In order therefore to revivify the system of capital movements from countries where capital is plentiful to territories where it is scarce, the essential conditions are an economic system which avoids recurrent world-wide depressions and which provides an efficient mechanism for necessary adjustments in the balances of international payments. These two conditions have already been the subject of discussion in Chapters III and IV. If the mechanism suggested in Chapter IV is adopted, individual nations will be free to adopt anti-depression policies and their balances of payments will be capable of adjustment by appropriate changes in exchange rates. In these conditions international capital movements might revive.

Should the International Authority take any steps to encourage or to control such movements?

Since such movements are in the general interest, the International Authority should be given powers to prevent any Member States from putting an embargo upon the issue of foreign loans in its capital market or upon the purchase of foreign securities or of other forms of property in foreign countries. In previous sections of this book reference has, however, been made to the fact that short-term speculative movements of capital serve no useful purpose. Such capital movements might be offset by the International Monetary Authority, as has been suggested in Chapter IV; and at the same time the Member States might themselves be left free to prevent such movements altogether, if they so desired, by means of exchange control on condition that the control was not used to limit other legitimate transactions. In order to prevent any such misuse of exchange controls, it might be necessary to give certain powers of supervision and regulation to the International Authority. This supervision would need to be used with care, since it is difficult in practice to distinguish in marginal cases between capital movements undertaken for legitimate commercial or economic investment and those undertaken to speculate on possible exchange fluctuations. It might be a sufficient solution of the problem to grant a right of appeal to the International Authority against the decision of the national authority of any Member State to veto any international capital transaction on the grounds of its speculative character.

The main difficulty in the application of such regulations would again arise in the case of completely "planned" economies. Where all capital is owned by the state and where all the community's savings are accumulated and invested by the state, "freedom" of international capital movements has no meaning; for the national authorities alone decide where capital is to be invested. Theoretically it is possible in the completely "planned" economy to measure the yield on capital invested at home, provided that proper use is made of a costing system of the kind discussed in Chapter II. For a comparison of the cost of new capital equipment with the price of the additional goods which that capital equipment is expected to produce should indicate the rate of return obtainable from such an investment. By comparing these internal yields with the interest obtainable on loans abroad the authorities in a "planned" economy could, if they wished, apply the principle of free capital movements. They could invest abroad whenever interest was higher abroad and borrow from abroad whenever interest was lower abroad than at home. It would, however, in practice be difficult for the International Authority to ensure that the national authorities in question adopted this principle. To do so would necessitate a very great extension of the powers of control of the International

Authority over the internal economic policy adopted in "planned" economic systems. Probably it could attempt little more than to encourage such capital movements on terms which were just and fair to lending and borrowing countries alike.

The International Authority might set up, in close contact with the International Bank to which reference has been made in Chapters III and IV, a special International Commission to supervise international capital movements. The main duties of such a body would be two-fold: first, to ensure that no Member States imposed restrictions on foreign lending with the exception of restrictions on speculative movements of short-term funds, and, secondly, to make sure that undeveloped territories were open as fields for investment on equal terms for all the Member States. It might, however, have certain subsidiary functions. It might supervise and give advice on the terms of international loan contracts. It might, for example, encourage the granting of such loans in the form of ordinary shares with dividends fluctuating according to profits instead of in the form of fixed-interest indebtedness; for this would greatly alleviate the problem of interest payments in case of any unavoidable economic depression in the borrowing country. If the monetary mechanism suggested in Chapter IV were adopted, it might encourage the use of the currency issued by the International Bank as the money in terms of which international loan contracts were fixed; for this might help to reduce the uncertainties for borrower and lender, resulting from the possibility of future fluctuations in the exchange value of debtor and creditor currencies. It might in certain cases investigate and report upon the profitability of various schemes of economic development which required the use of foreign capital, in order to prevent the investment of funds in excessive sums in any given direction or in schemes which were economically unjustifiable. It might perhaps supervise in various ways movements of capital between "liberal" and "planned" economies.

These are, however, subsidiary matters. The avoidance of trade depressions and the institution of an efficient mechanism for the adjustment of international balances of payments are the substantial conditions which in themselves would automatically revivify the flow of capital to the territories where it was most needed and most productive.

Chapter VII

EXCHANGE CONTROL AND CLEARING AGREEMENTS

BEFORE concluding the discussion of international trade and of international capital movements it is necessary to say something of various devices which have been developed in recent years for the national control of such international transactions. Of these devices the most important are exchange controls and clearing agreements, both of which mechanisms were adopted in the first place to relieve the strain on the balances of payments and the foreign exchanges of various countries. But in many cases they have been retained as instruments for the national control and planning of foreign trade, both for autarchic purposes — i.e. for the purpose of increasing national self-sufficiency through the protection and encouragement of essential industries at home —and also for the purpose, in some cases, of obtaining economic influence over other nations. It is important to determine what place, if any, such instruments of trade control would find in the International Organization.

It has already been shown in the previous

chapter that after 1929 the abrupt cessation of foreign lending by the creditor countries, the recall of short-term foreign loans already made by them, and the rapid decline in export prices placed an intolerable strain upon the balances of payments of many debtor countries. As an immediate measure to prevent this from leading to an excessive loss of gold or of other monetary reserves or to an excessive depreciation of the exchange value of their currencies, many debtor countries were driven to impose exchange controls with the limited object of preventing the export of capital. But it was soon found that, in order to control capital movements, a complete control over every form of foreign exchange transaction was necessary, and that a simple prohibition of the purchase of foreign currencies for the purpose of exporting capital was not sufficient. For there are many indirect ways in which capital may be exported. For example, exporters of commodities may use the foreign money which they obtain from the sale of their exports for investment in foreign countries instead of for the purchase of their own home currency; and by this means they can export part of their capital to foreign countries. For this reason a rigid control of capital transactions involves a strict supervision of the export trade. It necessitates also a strict control of imports; for importers who have purchased foreign currency for the ostensible purpose of buying foreign goods must be prevented from using these funds actually for investment of their capital abroad or for resale to foreigners who wish to repatriate capital which they had previously invested in the country in question.

For these reasons exchange controls which had been devised in the first place solely to prevent sudden capital exports were extended to cover all transactions in the purchase and sale of foreign currencies. With these fully developed systems of foreign exchange control the Central Bank or other monetary authority in the country in question was granted a monopoly of foreign exchange transactions. All purchases of foreign money for the finance of imports or other permissible transactions had to be made at the official exchange rate through the Central Bank; and all receipts of foreign money, whether from the sale of exports or from other sources, had to be surrendered at the official exchange rate to the Central Bank. By such means the export of capital could be reduced to a minimum.

But in most countries where this complete system of exchange control was developed, it was quickly used for other purposes than the control of capital movements. For the purposes of making the control effective it was necessary to rule that no goods could be imported without a permit from the monetary authorities to purchase the necessary foreign exchange; and this additional control of imports was soon used for protective purposes. This development seems to have occurred for two main reasons. In the first place, for various economic, social and strategic reasons many countries initiated a policy of autarchy during the post-1929 years. The planned development of home resources for the purpose of making the country as independent as possible of foreign supplies of foodstuffs, raw materials and essential manufactures required a strictly protective policy; and the control of imports through the regulation of foreign exchange permits presented a useful and effective addition to the armoury of protective weapons. But, secondly, a number of debtor countries were unable to restore equilibrium to their balances of payments simply by preventing the export of capital. For they had previously been actively borrowing from abroad; and something had to be done to offset the mere cessation of the grant of new loans. Moreover, the rapid decline in the world prices of the raw materials and foodstuffs which many of them exported led to a disastrous fall in their receipts from exports. This again needed the balancing factor of some restriction of imports or of some new stimulation of exports. Internal deflation of prices, costs and incomes was tried in many cases, but could not proceed rapidly or extensively enough. The depreciation of the gold value of their exchanges was avoided by many as a dangerous sign of financial weakness, or was insufficient in other cases to restore the balance. There remained only the method of direct restrictions of imports; and exchange control was therefore used to ration among the importers of essential commodities the available receipts of foreign money.

The far-reaching consequences of this development became clear only after the depreciation of the exchange values of the currencies of the main creditor countries which maintained free and uncontrolled dealings in foreign exchanges. The fall in the gold value of sterling in 1931, of the dollar in 1933 and of the French franc in 1936 reduced the gold value which could be obtained by the sale of the debtor countries' exports for sterling, dollars and francs; and this imposed a still greater burden upon the countries which still maintained officially the old gold values of their currencies. By means of increased restrictions upon imports, a number of the countries with exchange controls were still able to maintain a balance in their international payments in spite of the further decline in the gold value of their exports. But their internal price and cost structures, based upon currencies of the old gold value, became quite divorced from the price and cost structures of countries which had reduced the gold content of their currencies. And there were no forces still at work to remove this international disequilibrium, for the complete control of their foreign exchanges and the strict restriction of imports to correspond to the sums available for their finance removed the necessity either for an internal deflation of prices or for a depreciation in the exchange value of the currencies of the countries which maintained the old gold value of their money.

This divorce from world markets of many countries with exchange control led in its turn to the invention of various mechanisms for the promotion of their foreign trade. Without special aid trade with the countries with free exchanges became exceedingly difficult. For the exceptionally low gold prices which could be obtained from the sale of goods in the countries which had seriously reduced the gold values of their currencies made it unprofitable for producers in many countries with exchange controls to export to the countries with free exchanges. This led to a shortage of free-exchange currencies in the countries with exchange control, so that their imports from the countries with free exchanges had also to be reduced to very low levels. But trade between the various countries with exchange controls also became subject to peculiar difficulties. For the export of commodities to a country with exchange control resulted in the receipt by the exporter of a foreign currency whose exchange into his own currency was hedged about with many serious restrictions and difficulties. In this case exports were discouraged for fear that the payment for them might never be transferred into the seller's currency.

It was to avoid this latter difficulty that "exchange clearing agreements" were initiated between various countries with exchange controls or between a country with exchange control on the one hand and a country with free exchanges on the other. When an exchange clearing is started between two countries A and B, the importers in A pay the purchase price of their imports from B into a special account in A's currency; and the exporters in A are then paid directly from this special fund. The exporters in A must, if necessary, wait for payment until sufficient goods have been imported from B into A. Similarly exporters in B are paid from the sums accumulated in a special fund in B's currency as a result of purchases of A's goods by B. No pressure is exerted on either countries' foreign exchanges; for there are in fact no exchange dealings.

These agreements vary very much in detail according to their comprehensiveness. In some agreements payments for only a limited list of commodities have been effected through clearing accounts; in others payments for all commodity trade have been effected in this way; and in others payments for services such as tourist expenditure or interest payments have been made through the clearing accounts in addition to payments for commodity trade. In some agreements between exchange - control and free - exchange countries the method of what is called a "payments agreement" as opposed to that of an exchange clearing has been adopted. In this case the country with exchange control simply agrees to allot for the purchase of goods from the country with free exchanges at least a certain proportion of the money obtained by it from its exports to the country with free exchanges. But however much these agreements differ in detail or in form they have certain characteristics in common, the most important of which is to divert international trade into bilateral channels. With a strict clearing agreement the value of A's exports to B must be brought into an exact balance with B's exports to A in order that the clearing may function efficiently. With a payments agreement the bilateral balancing of trade may be less strict, but at least a certain rigidity is introduced; for A's exports to B are fixed in a definite relation to B's exports to A.

The development of such methods of financing international trade did not, however, remove the difficulties experienced in export markets by the countries which had maintained the old gold values of their currencies. As has already been seen, the official gold parities of their currencies were maintained by a number of countries by means of exchange controls in spite of the depreciation of the exchange value of the principal free-exchange currencies; and this, in the absence of a sufficiently extensive internal deflation of costs, made it practically impossible for some of the countries with exchange controls to sell their goods at a profitable gold price in the countries which had reduced the gold values of their currencies. To maintain their foreign trade they were obliged to take various measures to subsidize their exports. In some cases this was done directly by the payment of subsidies to exporters. In other cases exports were encouraged by arranging for the depreciation of the gold value of the controlled currency in certain circumstances and with certain conditions for the purpose of making it possible to undertake particular export transactions which would otherwise have been impossible. For example, potential purchasers of German goods were permitted in certain circumstances to purchase "blocked" marks of various kinds—e.g. marks owned by foreign creditors which were not allowed to be freely exchanged by the creditors—at a depreciated gold value. By such means foreigners were persuaded to buy German goods, which they would not have bought at their existing mark price unless marks had been obtainable at specially cheap rates.

Germany in fact presents the best illustration of a country which after 1929 went through the various stages of development which have been outlined in this chapter. The onset of the great depression was accompanied by a decline in demand in foreign markets, a rise in tariffs on German goods, a cessation of American lending to Germany and the recall of previously granted loans and credits by Germany's creditors. This placed a severe and abrupt strain on Germany's balance of payments; exchange control was introduced and was made more strict and rigid by successive stages. The currency was maintained at its old official gold value, partly as a result of memories of the rapid depreciation of the mark during the inflation of the early 1920's. In order to do so, however, the system of exchange control had to be used to restrict imports to correspond to the limited funds which were available for their purchase. The continued maintenance of the official gold value of the mark, even after the depreciation of such currencies as the pound sterling, the dollar and the French franc, completed the divorce between German prices and costs and world prices and costs.

The policy of rapid rearmament and internal economic expansion which was adopted by the National Socialist Government after 1933 necessitated an even closer control of the foreign exchanges and of foreign trade relations. For this plan of expansion naturally tended to cause a great increase in the demand for imports, and in particular for imported raw materials. If the gold value of the mark was still to be maintained, an even stricter control of imports was necessary; and this control was imposed by means of import boards which directly restricted and rationed the import of various commodities and by means of the foreign exchange control which administered the grant of permits to finance the purchase of imports. From this point in the development the controls of foreign trade were used more and more for the purposes of internal economic planning. In particular the "four year plan" had been devised to make Germany as self-sufficient as possible in vital raw materials by the production of substitute materials and by the exploitation of low-grade internal resources. The control of imports was used more and more for the express purpose of giving protection to such home industries. Moreover the rationing of the available imports of essential raw materials enabled the authorities to encourage those internal industries which were vital for the rearmament programme at the cost of withholding supplies from inessential civilian uses.

The divorce of internal German prices and costs from world prices made it extremely difficult for German producers to export without special aid. Exports had, however, to be maintained in order to finance the purchases of essential materials and foodstuffs from abroad. The measures taken have varied as between German trade with the free-exchange countries and German trade with other exchange-control countries, as is shown by the following passages taken from the League of Nations' *World Economic Survey*, 1938–39.[1]

In the case of her trade with countries with free-exchange systems, Germany has undertaken a number of measures to subsidize at various rates those exports

[1] (Series of League of Nations Publications. II. Economic and Financial, 1939. II. A. 18), pages 199–206.

which could not otherwise be effected. This is done either by varying degrees of direct subsidization or by depreciating to a varying extent the cost of the mark in terms of foreign currencies for certain export transactions.

The turnover of industrial undertakings is subjected to a levy, the height of which is not published, in order to raise funds for the direct subsidization of exports. The price of German bonds are considerably higher inside Germany than in foreign markets, where the receipt of interest from them is restricted by the German foreign-exchange control; and the resulting profit obtainable from the repatriation of Germany's external debt has been used to subsidize exports. Various "blocked marks," representing, for example, sums due to external debtors, may, on certain conditions, be exchanged into foreign currencies at a value considerably below the official value of the mark; and the profit which accrues to the monetary authorities from the purchase of foreign exchange with marks at their full official value and its sale for "blocked" marks of various degrees of depreciation is also used for the subsidization of particular exports.

The methods which Germany adopted in the case of trade with other countries with exchange controls are typified by her commercial relations with the countries of South-Eastern Europe and of Latin America:

The various methods which Germany has used to extend her trade with these countries have been based upon the existence of exchange control. With the countries of South-Eastern Europe, Germany has clearing agreements; and she was thus able to purchase freely the primary products of these countries without placing any strain on her foreign-exchange position.

For, in the event of an excess of German purchases, the exporters of South-Eastern Europe accumulated frozen balances of marks due to them in the clearing; and they could not obtain payment in their own currency until greater sums of their currency were paid into the clearing in the purchase of increased imports of German goods. . . .

In the early years of these clearing agreements, there was a large accumulation of frozen debts owed by Germany; but there is evidence that these balances have subsequently been reduced.[1] In order to reduce these debts, however, the countries of South-Eastern Europe have been obliged to increase their purchases of German products, often at the expense of similar or competing products of other countries.

Much the same method has been adopted by Germany for the expansion of trade in Latin America. The German importer pays the Latin-American exporter with "Aski" marks, which can be used only for the finance of German exports to the country from which Germany has imported. These "Aski" marks are sold by the Latin-American exporter at a value which is sufficiently depreciated to give the importer an inducement to purchase German goods. By this system also Germany could import freely from these countries, and an excess of imports would lead only to an accumulation of "Aski" marks which could be reduced only by increased purchases of German goods by the country in question.

A number of countries have, however, restricted their exports to Germany from time to time as an alternative method of preventing the accumulation of frozen balances of marks.

In the two previous chapters of this book the

[1] Cf. *The Economist*, December 3, 1938, page 485.

regulation of foreign trade and of international capital movements was discussed at some length in the cases of the "liberal" economies and also of the completely socialist economies in which, as in the U.S.S.R., foreign trade becomes a strict government monopoly. For both cases an attempt was made to outline the principles upon which international trade and international capital movements should be ordered. The trading system of the German type, however, conforms to neither of these two patterns. On the one hand, foreign trade has not been turned purely and simply into a government monopoly; but, in view of the system of subsidies, blocked marks of different rates of depreciation, import controls, clearing agreements and exchange control, the basis of the system cannot be said to remain "liberal." To what extent would such devices as clearing agreements and exchange controls be permissible instruments of regulation for the Member States of the International Organization? To what extent do the conclusions of Chapters V and VI require modification in the light of these trading methods?

From the point of view of the International Organization the adoption of such methods involves certain clear and definite disadvantages. In Chapter V it was argued that goods should be sold at prices equal to their costs of production, and that each country should purchase its requirements where they can be obtained most cheaply and should sell its products in the markets where consumers are offering the highest prices; for in this way the various countries will concentrate on the production of the goods which they are best fitted to make and consumers' requirements will be satisfied as efficiently as possible. The type of foreign trade control which has been examined in this chapter obviously offends against this "free trade" principle.

But in addition there are certain special dis-advantages which arise from the adoption of measures of this kind. The system of clearing agreements leads, as has been seen, to a strict balancing of trade between the two countries concerned; and this diversion of international trade from natural multilateral channels into strictly bilateral channels may cause a consider-able and unnecessary reduction in standards of living. An example will show the importance of this consideration. Country A may desire the products of country B; country B may desire those of country C; and country C those of country A. In a natural system of international trade, in which the relative prices and costs of the different goods in the different countries determine the course of trade, A will import from B, who will import from C, who will import from A. The *total* exports of each of the three countries may thus be brought into a balance with its *total* imports—A's imports from B, for example, being balanced by her exports to C—

even though there is no bilateral balance of trade between any single pair of countries. If a system of trading is then introduced which demands the bilateral balancing of trade between each pair of countries, the mutual advantages of the trade will be greatly diminished.

The disadvantages of any system of strict bilateralism extend also to transactions other than those for commodity imports and exports. For example, in the years before 1929 interest on investments in the Dominions and the Colonial Empire was transferred to the United Kingdom in part indirectly through multilateral channels. The Dominions and Colonies sold their raw materials and foodstuffs to many countries of Europe, such as Germany; and the United Kingdom purchased special manufactured articles from these European countries. The excess of exports of the Dominions and Colonies to Germany, and Germany's excess of exports to the United Kingdom enabled the Dominions and Colonies to extend their export markets and to pay their debts with a minimum of difficulty; it helped Germany to obtain necessary raw materials in exchange for her exports to the United Kingdom; and it made it possible for the United Kingdom to receive the interest on its overseas investments in the form of the goods which it most desired. The adoption of bilateral clearing agreements by Germany and other countries of Europe, together with the extension of imperial preferences throughout the British Commonwealth in the Ottawa agreements of 1932, drove these transactions into bilateral channels; and the United Kingdom in more recent years has received payment of interest more directly by means of a greater excess of imports from the rest of the British Commonwealth. With this change the substantial gains which resulted from the multilateral method of payment have been lost to the disadvantage of all the parties concerned.

Proposals have been made from time to time for extending the system of bilateral clearing agreements into a system of multilateral exchange clearing. With such a system each of the countries concerned would compel its importers to pay into a clearing account all the sums payable in respect of its imports from any of the other countries adhering to the system; and the national currency of each country which was accumulated in this way in the clearing account would be used to pay to its exporters for the sale of goods to any of the other countries making use of the common clearing. With such a system there would still be no actual exchange of one national currency into another; but at the same time multilateral transactions would be possible. Each country's imports from any particular country need no longer balance precisely with its exports to that country.

In order that full advantage should be taken of the possibilities of multilateral transactions, it is clear that such a system of a multilateral exchange clearing would need to be universal. That is to say (a) it should include as many countries as possible and (b) international transactions of every kind—e.g. for interest payments, for financial, shipping and tourist services, and for capital movements—should be payable through the multilateral clearing. Only such transactions as speculative transfers of short-term capital, which it was desired to prevent entirely, should be excluded. The Member States of the International Organization might set up a multilateral exchange clearing of this kind. If this were done, some mechanism would have to be devised for ensuring that the total payments of each Member State into the clearing was equal to its total receipts from the clearing; for unless this were so, Member States whose receipts from other Member States were greater than their payments to those other States would accumulate credits in the clearing which could not be transferred into their own currency. In other words, such a system still requires some mechanism for adjusting the balance of payments between the countries concerned.

It would be possible to preserve this balance by a direct restriction of imports in the case of any Member State which was accumulating debts to other Member States in the clearing; but if—in the interests of the principle of free trade—this method of readjustment is excluded, it would become necessary to alter the rates of exchange between the various national currencies for this purpose. Thus, for example, a Member State which was accumulating a debit balance in the clearing which could not be transferred to its creditors should be obliged to lower the price at which its currency was reckoned in terms of the currencies of the other Member States. This would have the effect of lowering the price of its exports in the other currencies, and of raising the price of its imports in its own currency; and the consequent stimulation of its exports and reduction of its imports would enable it to reduce its debit balance in the clearing account.

A system of this kind would offend against none of the free trade principles, and at the same time would provide an efficient and flexible instrument for keeping the balance of payments of the various Member States in equilibrium; but it has no particular advantages over the system outlined in Chapter IV. Indeed, a multilateral and universal clearing, in which the exchange rates between the various currencies are adjusted to offset accumulations of untransferred debits or credits in the clearing, is for practical purposes identical with a system in which the various Member States buy and sell freely in world markets and adjust the exchange values of their currencies to offset an export or an import of monetary reserves. On general principles there is nothing to choose between two systems which are so similar.

Bilateral clearing agreements, we have seen,

are open to the special objection that they eliminate the advantages which can often be obtained
from a system of multilateral trade. Special
objections can also be raised against various other
features of the type of trading system which was
described in earlier sections of this chapter. The
direct subsidization of exports and the use of
"blocked" currencies of varying degrees of depreciation, as methods of stimulating exports, are
open to grave misuse. The country which adopts
these methods is tempted to pay a heavy subsidy
on the export of certain goods to a particular
market where competition is keen, but to pay no
subsidy and so to exact a high price for the same
goods in markets which for one reason or another
are more secure. Alternatively, potential purchasers may be permitted to obtain "blocked"
balances of the exporting country's currency at
a cheap and much depreciated rate, if this is
necessary in order to tempt them to make their
purchases; and at the same time purchasers of
the same goods in other markets may be obliged
to obtain the exporting country's currency at the
official and more expensive rate, if there is little
danger that this will prevent the purchase from
being made.

This system of paying varying rates of subsidy
for different goods and in different markets has
two special disadvantages from the international
point of view. In the first place, it prevents the
best use being made of the productive resources

of the country which employs these devices. If, for example, the country pays a heavy subsidy on product A and no subsidy on product B, this will encourage foreign consumers to purchase much of A and little of B. They will continue to buy A until the satisfaction which they obtain from the last units of it is small, but they will stop purchasing B when the satisfaction obtainable from additional units of it is still relatively high. If both commodities were put on the market at prices which corresponded to their costs, consumers would purchase less A and more B; and they would thus get a greater total satisfaction from the output of the same productive resources of the exporting country. Another type of waste may arise if the exporting country sells the same commodity at a low price to country X and at a high price to country Y. Consumers in X may be tempted by the low price to purchase it in such quantities that the last units of it give them relatively little satisfaction; and consumers in Y may be compelled by the high price to halt their purchases at a point at which much satisfaction could still be gained from additional purchases. If the selling price was the same in both markets, more would be purchased in Y and less in X, so that the consumers as a whole would obtain a greater total satisfaction from the same volume of production. In fact, for reasons of this kind, the most satisfactory use of productive resources will be made only if all products are made available to all consumers on equal terms at prices which correspond to the costs of production of the various goods. The type of trading system which we have been examining in this chapter clearly offends against this rule.

But there is a second special reason for dis-allowing such measures. Discrimination in the selling prices charged for its exports may enable an important exporting country to gain an advantage at the expense of the exploitation of its weaker and smaller customers. High prices can be charged to the smaller and weaker countries, which for one reason or another have the smallest power of retaliation. This state of affairs is not only undesirable in itself; but from the point of view of determining the most stable economic foundations for international peace this type of action is open to special objections. The sense of injustice which is bred from such inequalities of economic treatment and the concentration of the aggrieved victims upon measures of retaliation create an atmosphere which is particularly un-favourable for the development of a durable peace system.

Indeed, the main objection to the whole type of commercial policy outlined in this chapter is that it may cause international trade to degene-rate into a chaotic and unregulated form of warfare instead of being a purely economic acti-vity carried out on straightforward and simple rules to the mutual benefit of all the countries concerned. If the methods outlined in this chapter are adopted by an important country, that country may thereby be able to exercise an economic domination over other smaller countries. It may, for example, attempt to gain a partial monopoly in certain channels of foreign trade by purchasing heavily from a small country with which it has a clearing agreement; for the small country will then be obliged to divert its purchases from other countries in order to clear off the untransferred credits which are owed to it in the clearing. But such economic domination, once it has been achieved, may be used for the exertion of political and diplomatic pressure; for a threat on the part of the important trading country abruptly to curtail its trade with the weaker country might be disastrous to that country, even though it would effect only a relatively small part of the stronger country's trade.

As far as the economic relations between the important trading countries themselves are concerned, the adoption of the type of system outlined in this chapter leads to equally objectionable results. By imperceptible stages each government may be led on in a series of retaliatory acts to a state of open economic warfare. Preferential duties, discriminating rates of export subsidy and rigorously bilateral commercial agreements will be used to monopolize particular markets; and the threat to boycott particular markets for exports or imports will be used to intimidate the weaker or to defy the stronger trading rivals. It is for these reasons in particular that the system outlined in Chapters IV and V above is to be recommended. If each country buys and sells its goods at uniform prices which correspond to their costs of production, and if the balance of international payments of each country is adjusted by a regulation of the exchange value of its currency at a uniform rate for all transactions and for all other countries, international trade can be conducted in a way that brings a mutual advantage without any possibility of serious discrimination. Moreover, such a system would provide a set of fairly simple rules capable of being interpreted and administered impartially. On such a basis an economic peace could be constructed.

For these reasons, the type of trading system examined in this chapter should be forbidden by the International Authority. But the abolition of exchange controls and of clearing agreements as instruments for the regulation of international trade would probably need to be undertaken gradually. Just as in Chapter V it was suggested that the sudden abolition of all tariff barriers might lead to very serious problems of "special" unemployment, for the same reasons too abrupt an elimination of exchange controls and of bilateral clearing agreements would be dangerous. The International Authority must therefore regulate the speed at which these devices should be abandoned. It would be possible, for example, in the case of exchange control to rule that gradually increasing proportions of all transactions should be freed from control. For example, exporters might be allowed to sell a certain proportion of the money proceeds of their exports to potential importers in a free exchange market, and they would be obliged to sell only the remaining proportion at the fixed official rate to the national monetary authority. By raising the free proportion of foreign exchange the control could be gradually eliminated. In the case of clearing agreements a similar method could be adopted. Exporters might be free to use a certain proportion of the proceeds of their exports as they liked, and might be obliged to pay only the remaining proportion into the clearing. Again, by successive increases in the free proportion of foreign exchange the clearing could be gradually abandoned.

The abandonment of exchange controls and bilateral clearing agreements as devices for the regulation of international trade does not mean that Member States would not be free, if they so wished, to control their trading relations with other states in various ways in order to facilitate any type of internal economic planning which they had adopted. The various controls which they would be permitted to exercise have been mentioned in different sections of the preceding chapters; but it may be useful to recapitulate them here.

(1) Any Member State would be permitted to

set up a complete system of foreign exchange control, under which all foreign exchange transactions were monopolized by the national monetary authority, provided that it was used only to prevent speculative movements of short-term capital. That is to say, the national monetary authority would have to buy and sell foreign exchange in unrestricted quantities at the official rate for all transactions other than short-term capital movements, and the official rate of exchange would be subject to revision to maintain equilibrium in the country's balance of payments.

(2) Any Member State would be permitted to set up a national import or export board to control the imports or exports of any particular commodity; and any Member State would be permitted to monopolize the whole of its foreign trade in a single national foreign trade board. These import and export boards or foreign trade boards would, moreover, be permitted to plan ahead the foreign trade of the country in the sense of fixing by long-term contracts the quantity of goods to be imported from or exported to any particular markets. These foreign trade plans would, however, be subjected to periodic revision under the supervision of the International Authority, on the principles that imports and exports should be purchased and sold at uniform prices in the different foreign markets and should be adjusted in total quantity so as to equate home prices and costs with foreign prices and costs.

(3) Any Member State would be permitted to use the instrument of direct subsidization to different home industries in order to encourage any occupations which it was desired to expand for social or other non-economic reasons.

With such a system a reasonable compromise might be achieved between a uniform international economic system and the desire of different Member States to adopt different national economic policies; but nothing less radical than international regulation of the kind suggested would probably suffice to ensure that international trade could not degenerate into a form of economic warfare.

Chapter VIII

INTERNATIONAL POPULATION MOVEMENTS

THERE are certain regions of the world which are rich in raw materials and in land but which are still comparatively undeveloped. In a number of these areas, such as Australia, New Zealand and certain of the republics of South America, the full development of the existing resources requires not only a greater capital equipment, but also a larger working population. The United States of America is in a different position. For it is not only rich in natural resources and fertile land, but is also abundantly supplied with capital equipment; there is, however, a relative scarcity of population in the sense that there is considerably less labour per unit of capital and natural resources than in other fully developed countries such as the United Kingdom, France or Germany.

In contrast to these countries in which population is comparatively scarce, there are a number of others in which there is a comparative scarcity of raw materials or of capital in relation to an abundant population. Many of the countries of Asia, such as Japan, India and China, are in this position; and in some of these countries, as in India, there is, in the view of a number of authorities, a real pressure of population upon the available means of subsistence. In other regions of the world such as in Eastern and Southern Europe there are countries with an abundance of population in relation to the available capital and natural resources; and Poland, Italy and some of the Balkan countries may be placed within this group. Among these there are some, such as Italy, where there are no rich natural resources. In such cases progress must depend either upon further industrialization, based on capital development and the import of raw materials and the export of finished products, or else upon a reduction of population. In other cases, such as some of the Balkan countries, there are probably rich natural resources to be exploited and many improvements to be introduced into agriculture and industrial technique. In these cases population can be said to be excessive only in relation to the existing capital equipment, to the existing degree of exploitation of natural resources and to the existing level of technical knowledge and training.

It is clear that there is great diversity in the conditions of population in the various countries. Nevertheless, it is possible to divide countries into two broad categories—those in which there is a relative scarcity of population and those in which population is abundant or even excessive in relation to the other available sources of production.

The productivity of labour is likely to be high in the first type of country, where each worker will be working with an abundant amount of capital equipment and natural resources; and for this reason the real wage-rate offered for labour is likely to be comparatively high. On the other hand, in the countries with a relative scarcity of natural resources and of capital equipment the productivity of labour is likely to be low; and the competition of the abundant labour supply in the search for work is likely to reduce real wage-rates to a comparatively low level. In so far as labour is able and willing to move from one country to another there is likely to be a migration of population from the relatively over-populated to the relatively underpopulated territories in search of higher wages.

From the international point of view such migration brings with it two important economic advantages, comparable to the advantages which, as was seen above in Chapter VI, should accrue from a free international movement of capital. In the first place, the movement of labour from a territory where its productivity is low to a territory where its productivity is high will increase total world production. For this reason, migration of population from relatively over-populated to relatively underpopulated countries is one factor which should help to raise the general level of economic well-being. The second economic advantage to be gained from such movements is that they help to diminish the great inequalities which at present exist between the standards of living in different countries. The emigration of labour from a poor and relatively overpopulated country, by easing the labour market there, will tend to raise the wages and the standard of living of its workers towards the levels achieved in the countries of immigration. In fact, there are only four fundamental ways of raising the standard of living in the poor and overpopulated countries: by greater freedom of international trade which will extend the markets of such countries; by the investment of foreign capital in them; by an increase in their technical skill and training; and by a diminution in the pressure of their populations upon the available resources. The first three of these methods have been discussed in previous chapters; it is the main purpose of this chapter to inquire to what extent emigration of their population can and should be used as a method of raising their standard of living.

It is necessary to realize that there *may* be a real conflict of interest between the countries of emigration and the countries of immigration. Emigration from a densely populated territory will raise the standard of living in that territory by relieving the pressure of population. Immigration into a country with a high standard of living *may* reduce the standard of living in that country by increasing the working population in relation to the available resources of land and capital, and thereby reducing the productivity of labour in the country in question.

This result is not, however, certain. If the country of immigration is seriously underpopulated, it is possible that a growth of population will actually raise productivity and the standard of living. For if the working population is too small, production on a large scale will be impossible and all the modern technical advantages which can be obtained from the utilization of methods of mass production will be lost. In such cases a growth of population might lead to a rise in output per head by giving scope to the economies of mass production, even if the available resources of capital equipment and of land remained unchanged so that each worker was somewhat less well equipped. For this reason migration from a seriously overpopulated to a seriously underpopulated country will, in the long run, raise the standard of living in both countries.

But even in such cases the standard of living may be reduced temporarily in the country of immigration in those trades and occupations in which the immigrant workers find it most easy to gain their first footing. For the consequent overcrowding in these occupations will lead to reduced wages in them. In the cases in which there is no serious underpopulation in the country of immigration there will be no need for a growth of population to enable the country to reap the benefits of large-scale production; and in these cases the immigration of foreign labour may permanently keep the standard of living somewhat below the level which it might otherwise have reached. Although it is true in all cases that the migration of labour from a country of low labour productivity to one of high labour productivity will increase total world production, yet the fact that workers in the country of immigration may stand to lose from the movement gives rise to considerable pressure for the prevention of immigration into the richer countries. Because of the conflict of national interests between countries of emigration and of immigration, international migration is particularly in need of regulation by an impartial International Authority. But if the International Authority is given power of decision in this question, on what principles should it act?

To answer this question it will be useful to examine shortly the existing population trends in different areas of the world; for at the present time there is a certain disharmony in these population movements. Generally speaking, it is in those countries in which population is already relatively most abundant that the most rapid growth of population seems likely to occur in the future. The figures in the first column of the following table give some indication of this fact:

	Net Reproduction Rate	Expectation of Life at Birth (Number of Years: Females only)
Japan	1·57 (1930)	47 (1926–30)
India	— —	27 (1931)
Bulgaria	1·19 (1933–36)	47 (1925–28)
Italy	1·13 (1935–37)	56 (1930–32)
Poland	1·11 (1934)	51 (1931–32)
New Zealand ..	1·02 (1938)	68 (1931)
U.S.A. (whites only)	0·95 (1936)	64 (1936)
Germany	0·93 (1936)	63 (1932–34)
France	0·87 (1937)	59 (1928–33)
England and Wales	0·78 (1937)	64 (1937)
Sweden	0·76 (1936)	65 (1931–35)

(Figures taken from the *Statistical Year-Book of the League of Nations*, 1938–39. London: George Allen & Unwin, Ltd.)

Population growth—apart from international migration—depends upon the balance between births and deaths; and in order to compare the forces of fertility and mortality it might seem most natural to compare the crude birth-rates and death-rates in the different countries. But these rates are often misleading. Suppose, for example, that at any particular time a given population temporarily contains an abnormally high percentage of persons of reproductive age and an abnormally low percentage of the very young and the very old. This population will show an abnormally low death-rate—since mortality is heaviest among the very young and the very old—and an abnormally high birth-rate as a result of the abnormally high proportion of persons in the reproductive ages. For these reasons the net reproduction rate has been used in the above table to illustrate the balance between the forces of fertility and mortality in the different countries. This rate measures the extent to which a given population is reproducing itself at the current mortality and fertility rates, and is not affected by the actual age-distribution of the population.[1] Thus the net reproduction rate of 1·57 for Japan in 1930 shows that if mortality and fertility rates at different ages were stabilized at the 1930 level, the population of Japan would eventually increase by 57 per cent in each generation; and, at the other end of the scale, the net reproduction rate of 0·76 for Sweden in 1936 shows that if mortality and fertility remained constant at the 1936 level, the Swedish population would eventually reproduce only 76 per cent of itself in each generation.

One striking feature stands out clearly from this table. It is precisely in those countries of Asia and of Eastern and Southern Europe—such as Japan, Bulgaria, Italy and Poland—in which conditions already to-day approximate most nearly to those of relative overpopulation, that the net reproduction rate is highest. In fact, it is precisely

[1] It is calculated by reckoning the number of female infants which will be left behind by 1,000 existing female infants, as these latter grow up and produce babies at the current rates of fertility and die off at the current rates of mortality. If 1,000 female babies will leave 1,500 potential mothers behind them, the net Reproduction Rate is said to be 1·50.

in these countries that the forces of fertility in recent years have been stronger than those of mortality, so that the underlying tendency is for a continued increase in population; and in Japan, as can be seen from the table, this rate of increase is likely to continue to be high.

In certain relatively underpopulated areas, among which may be numbered New Zealand, Australia, and perhaps the United States of America,[1] the underlying forces of mortality and fertility have been fairly evenly balanced in recent years, although, as the table shows, there is some indication that the forces of fertility have already become weaker than those of mortality. In other countries of Western Europe which fall between these two categories of underpopulated and over-populated countries—such as Germany, France, England and Wales, and Sweden—fertility has already fallen considerably below mortality; and, indeed, in England and Wales and in Sweden at current fertility and mortality the population would eventually decline by 20 to 25 per cent in each generation.

This situation has been brought about in the countries of Western European civilization by the very considerable decline in fertility which has recently occurred. Mortality has also fallen as a

---

[1] Unfortunately there is not sufficient evidence to determine the position in the republics of South America, some of which with suitable exploitation might also provide room for a considerably greater population.

result of improvements in hygiene, nutrition and public health; but fertility has fallen even more rapidly. The following figures for certain Anglo-

Net Reproduction Rates

Australia ..	..	1·32 (1920–22)	0·99 (1937)
New Zealand	..	1·29 (1921–22)	1·02 (1938)
U.S.A. (white population)		1·08 (1930)	0·95 (1936)

Saxon countries show how quickly the net reproduction rate has declined in recent years as a result of this rapid fall in fertility. If this tendency should continue, the threat of a population decline in some of the most important territories of potential immigration will become even more real.

It is possible that this existing disharmony in the rate of growth of population in the relatively overpopulated and the relatively underpopulated countries will, in part at least, be resolved in the future by a fall in fertility in the countries in which population growth is now comparatively high. The social environment and outlook which has accompanied the rise of standards of living in the countries of Western European civilization and which has led to the rapid decline of fertility in these areas may well spread to other areas. In the long run it is possible that this development may provide the fundamental solution of the problem. But there is reason to believe that it cannot rapidly become effective. For so radical a change in social habit will necessarily take a considerable time to develop.

Moreover, it is precisely in the countries in which fertility is highest that there is the greatest scope for a reduction in mortality. As the second column of the table on page 147 shows, the expectation of life of a female infant in India is only some thirty years and in Japan and Bulgaria only some fifty years. In these cases there are great possibilities of reducing mortality by means of improved nutrition, improved hygiene and improved medical treatment in general.

Any reduction in fertility, therefore, which may occur in the future in these countries is likely to be accompanied for some time by an equivalent reduction in mortality. On the other hand, in the countries of Western European civilization, as the table on page 147 shows, the expectation of life at birth has already been raised to between sixty and seventy years. It is true that some further reductions in mortality may still be expected in these countries, particularly as a result of improved nutritional and health services among the poorer sections of the community. But the possibilities are much more limited in these countries; and reduced mortality can make only a small contribution towards the prevention of the threatened decline in numbers.[1]

[1] In England and Wales, for example, it has been calculated that at the rates of fertility ruling in 1937 the population would reproduce only 88 per cent of itself in each generation even if *no*

India may perhaps be taken as an exceptionally clear case of a country in which the population problem is of great importance. The population is still increasing at a fairly rapid rate, having risen from 315 millions in 1911 to 353 millions in 1931. There is at the same time already considerable overpopulation; and some authorities can see evidence of an actual pressure of population upon the available means of physical subsistence.[1] A high birth-rate is matched by a high death-rate. There is a high density of population; and agricultural holdings are often uneconomically small. The standard of living is so low that little reserves exist, and crop failures bring death from famine and disease. The expectation of life, as has been seen, is peculiarly low; and the actual increase in population which is taking place is probably made possible only through the extension of the physical means of subsistence by irrigation works and similar public development. Increased economic opportunities, in fact, seem to be used up through an increase in the population at its existing low standards rather than through a rise in the standard of living for the existing population.

potential mothers were to die between birth and the end of their reproductive period. Corresponding figures for other countries in recent years are as follows: New Zealand (1938) 111 per cent, Australia (1937) 108 per cent, United States of America (white population only: 1935) 101 per cent, Germany (1936) 106 per cent, France (1936) 101 per cent, and Sweden (1936) 84 per cent.

[1] Cf. Carr-Saunders, *World Population*, pages 271–75.

In such conditions improved medical services, by reducing mortality from disease and so increasing the existing pressure of population, might lead merely to an increased mortality from famine and malnutrition. Even large-scale emigration, if it were possible, would cause no permanent cure so long as the consequent reduction of population pressure led merely to a more rapid growth of population to fill the empty places. In such cases decreased fertility alone provides a basic cure. But it must be realized that it is precisely in conditions such as those of India that decreased fertility and higher standards of living will for a long time be accompanied by decreased mortality. Moreover, it so happens that in India there are certain ancient social customs which themselves diminish the fertility of women; child marriage leads to premature death or loss of fecundity, and the prohibition on the remarriage of widows restricts births. A reorientation of social environment would probably lead to the revision of such customs and this in itself would be another factor tending to increase the pressure of population in the absence of fresh checks upon fertility.[1]

The above paragraphs should serve to make clear the lack of balance which exists in the divergent trends of population in certain regions of the world. Some of the important countries in which there is relative overpopulation are still

[1] Cf. Carr-Saunders, op. cit., pages 276–77.

threatened with a considerable increase in numbers; in some of the important countries in which there is relative underpopulation the population will soon cease to grow and will probably decline. One obvious solution for this lack of balance is suggested by the migration of people from the former to the latter regions. In fact, during the nineteenth century emigration, first from Western Europe and later from Southern and Eastern Europe, to North America and, to a lesser extent, to South America and to the British Dominions, played an important role in relieving population pressures. But directly after the war of 1914–18 serious obstacles to such migration were imposed in the countries of immigration; and with the development of the great depression after 1929 these obstacles were substantially increased as a result of the growth of unemployment among the existing working populations in the countries of potential immigration.

As the following passage shows, these obstacles have in fact been most severe precisely in those cases in which migration might have served most to relieve existing population pressures:

The serious reduction in the volume of migration since the beginning of the century is due to the severe restrictions which many countries have imposed upon immigration. During the last years of the nineteenth and the first years of the twentieth century, the United States of America and the British Dominions, which with the countries of South America provided the greatest opportunities for immigration, closed their doors to Chinese and Japanese immigrants, and indeed practically to all Asiatic immigrants.

Restriction of immigration has been applied by the United States and the British Dominions to European immigrants as well. The Quota Acts of the United States, passed in 1921 and 1924, greatly restricted immigration. While immigration from countries to which the quota is applied had averaged over 800,000 per annum in the years 1900–1914, total annual immigration from these countries was fixed at a maximum of 357,803 as a result of the Act of 1921 and 153,774 as a result of the Act of 1924. But these Acts discriminated severely in favour of migrants from the United Kingdom and from Northern and Western Europe as opposed to those coming from Eastern and Southern Europe. For example, the Italian quota was fixed at 3,845 and the Polish quota at 6,524, which figures may be compared with an annual average immigration of some 200,000 Italians into the United States during the years 1900–14 and with an immigration of some 95,000 Poles into the United States in 1921. Immigration into Canada, Australia, New Zealand and the Union of South Africa is also strictly controlled; and these controls have been used to discriminate, first, in favour of British immigrants and, secondly, in many cases in favour of immigrants from the north and west as opposed to the east and south of Europe. The countries of Central and Southern America have restricted immigration by the strict control of visas; and a serious limitation on European immigration is imposed by a clause of the Federal Constitution of Brazil, which limits immigration for each nationality to 2 per cent of the number of immigrants of that nationality who have settled in Brazil during the last fifty years.

In short, practically all important countries of immigration except some countries of South America exclude Asiatics; and many important countries of immigration discriminate severely in favour of migrants from Western and Northern Europe as opposed to migrants from Eastern and Southern Europe. But it is precisely in Northern and Western Europe that a population decline is imminent; and it is in Southern and Eastern Europe and in certain countries of Asia that there is most evidence of over-population and the likelihood of a continuation of rapid population growth.[1]

There are inevitably a number of serious obstacles to international migration. Language difficulties and the ties of sentiment, custom and culture restrain men and women from leaving their home countries. Ignorance of conditions and opportunities abroad and the cost of transport impede such movement, even if men are otherwise ready to move. Finally, as we have seen, severe artificial obstacles have been erected by the governments of the countries of immigration. In view of these facts what policy should the International Authority adopt in its control of international migration? Should it free migration from all artificial barriers? Should it go further and encourage migration by disseminating information about conditions in the countries of immigration and by providing special facilities for movement? On the other hand, should it itself impose restrictions on migration; and, if so, on what principles?

From the world economic point of view there

[1] Cf. League of Nations' *World Economic Survey*, 1938–39 (Series of League of Nations Publications. II. Economic and Financial, 1939. II. A. 18), pages 165 and 166.

can be little doubt that migration should be positively encouraged from countries of low labour productivity to countries of high productivity; and from the purely economic point of view there is only one serious qualification of this principle to be made. Emigration should not be freely permitted from a country in which an existing pressure of population upon the means of subsistence is maintained as a result of excessive and unchecked fertility in that country. For, in the first place, as we have already seen, emigration would provide no permanent cure for the pressure of population at home, since the empty places would quickly be refilled; and, secondly, there would logically be no end to such emigration until all the possible countries of immigration had themselves been overpopulated by this unchecked source of immigrants.

The problem is, however, not solely an economic one. The migration of a people into an alien land raises psychological, biological and social problems of the greatest importance. It may be difficult or impossible to assimilate two peoples of different racial and cultural characteristics in the same country, particularly if the migration proceeds too rapidly. It is no part of the purpose of this book to pass judgment upon such non-economic problems. They may, nevertheless, be considered by the International Authority as providing valid reasons for limiting or even prohibiting certain population movements.

Certain broad conclusions can, however, be drawn from the purely economic considerations which have been discussed in this chapter. There can be little doubt that the International Authority should, for economic reasons, insist on a greater freedom for international migration than exists at present. It should, however, do all that is within its power to encourage the control of their population growths by the various Member States, in order to check fertility in relatively overpopulated countries which are threatened with further serious increases in numbers and to raise fertility in the relatively underpopulated countries which are threatened with a decline in numbers. The actual regulations of international migration should, moreover, be closely related to these national population policies. For migration should properly be subjected to special restrictions in the case of emigration from countries in which population growth was excessive and uncontrolled; and immigration into an underpopulated country should be made particularly easy if the existing population in that country is not fully reproducing itself.

Chapter IX

COLONIES AND RAW MATERIAL SUPPLIES

IT has frequently been stated that countries which do not possess colonial territories for exploitation are economically at a disadvantage in comparison with the countries with colonial empires; and in particular it is argued that the absence of colonial possessions makes it difficult for certain countries to obtain adequate supplies of raw materials. These questions may be examined in the light of the economic principles which have been discussed in the foregoing chapters. To what extent does the possession of colonies confer economic advantages? On what economic principles should colonial territories be administered? In what way might supplies of raw materials—whether they be produced in colonial territories or not—be made equally accessible to the different countries?

Colonial territories are of economic importance in various ways. They provide markets for exports, and sources from which raw materials and foodstuffs may be imported; the capital development of colonial territories opens up new sources of supply of colonial products, provides an additional demand for machinery and other capital goods and offers a profitable field for the investment of capital; to a limited extent colonial territories may offer an outlet for the emigration of population.

These advantages may be somewhat more readily available to the countries possessing colonies than to those without colonies, even if there is no legal discrimination in favour of the colonial power. In a British colony, for example, English will be the official language; the British administrators will have closer business contacts with other parts of the British Commonwealth than with other countries; the legal system and commercial habits are likely to be more familiar to the British than to persons of other nationalities; social habits in the colony will be more closely related to British customs than to those of other countries; and, finally, there will be closer ties of sentiment with the rest of the British Commonwealth than with other parts of the world. For all these various reasons the British will, in fact, obtain certain advantages from the territory. Importers in the United Kingdom, for example, may obtain the products of the colony rather more easily than importers in other countries, simply because there are no differences in language and commercial practice. Exporters in the United Kingdom may, for similar reasons, find easier access to the markets of the colony. The colonial administrators themselves may—perhaps almost unconsciously—give preferences to the

United Kingdom in their contracts for imported supplies or for works of public construction. At the same time the colony may be more readily available as a field for the investment of British capital and for the emigration of British labour than for investment and migration from other countries; for knowledge of opportunities in the colony will be more easily obtainable by the British and there will be a greater sense of security and of familiarity for the British in moving to a territory under British rule.

But special advantages of this kind would probably not be very substantial in the absence of legal preferences for the British. Legal equality of opportunity for the trade of other countries with the colony would ensure that the British could not obtain a substantially higher price or a much more extended market for their sales in the colony than could the exporters of similar products from other countries. Nor could the British obtain supplies from the colony on sub-stantially better terms than purchasers in other countries if the producers in the colony were free to sell their products to the highest bidder. If in addition the administrators in the colony are legally bound to accept the lowest-priced contracts for supplies and for works of public construction, and if no special legal obstacles are placed in the way of investment of capital and migration of labour from other countries, there will be no very great inequalities in the enjoyment of the economic benefits from colonial territories by the various nations.

The application of the "open-door" principle —i.e. the principle of legal and administrative equality of economic opportunity in colonial territories for all nations—should thus remove all the major *economic* grievances of the countries without colonies. The "open-door" principle is, moreover, to the advantage of the native inhabitants of the colony. Native interests may, for example, be prejudiced by duties or quotas on imports into the colony, which give a preference to the products of the mother country; for such discriminatory restrictions make it impossible for the inhabitants of the colony to purchase their supplies in the cheapest market. Similarly, duties on exports from the colony which discriminate in favour of the mother country may divert the sales of the native producers from their most profitable foreign markets. In fact, the "open-door" principle implies that goods may be purchased and capital may be borrowed by the colonial inhabitants in the cheapest available foreign markets, and that the colonial produce may be sold in the dearest market; and such a principle is clearly to the advantage of the colony itself.

We may conclude, therefore, that the International Authority should be able to determine the economic relations between colonial territories and other countries, and that it should ensure that the principle of the "open-door" is applied.

This solution of the economic problem is independent of the political principles which may be adopted for colonial administration. Thus the "open-door" principle may be applied to colonies the political administration of which is still completely controlled by the colonial powers; and, in fact, this regime is already applied to African colonies in the Congo basin by virtue of treaties which guarantee the "open-door" in that area. Alternatively, the "open-door" may be applied by the extension of the principle of the existing mandates of the League of Nations; for with this system the administration of a colonial territory is entrusted by an international body to a particular nation on certain conditions, which include the application of the "open-door" principle and which are designed to safeguard the interests both of the natives of the colony and of other sovereign countries. Finally, the "open-door" principle might be assured by handing over the colonial territories to the International Authority itself for actual administration by a competent international body. It is no part of the purpose of this book to discuss these political questions. From the purely economic point of view all that is essential is to ensure that the "open-door" principle is actually applied.

It has frequently been argued that countries which do not possess colonies are at a special disadvantage in obtaining essential raw material supplies. It is important, therefore, to examine how much force there is in this argument, and to what extent this particular problem would be solved by the application of the "open-door" principle to colonial territories. The question of raw material supplies is, however, considerably wider than the colonial problem. For while certain very important raw materials, such as rubber and tin, are produced entirely or largely in colonial territories, it has been calculated that the total production of all commercially important raw materials in all colonial territories was no more than about 3 per cent of world production in 1936.[1] We must, therefore, extend the inquiry and ask not only whether the application of the open-door principle to the colonies will solve the problem of colonial raw material supplies, but also whether the various suggestions made in the preceding chapters of this book will solve the problem of raw material supplies from non-colonial sources.

The problem of raw material supplies naturally falls under two heads. "On the one hand, difficulties were felt regarding the *supply* of raw materials—that is, certain countries considered that, even when they were in a position to pay for all the raw materials they required, they either could not obtain them at all or were compelled to pay what was in their view an excessively high price for them. On the other hand, certain

[1] Cf. League of Nations, *Report of the Committee for the Study of the Problem of Raw Materials*, 1937.

countries experienced principally difficulties in regard to *payment*—that is, they felt that, even when ample supplies were available, they themselves were, for reasons beyond their own control, unable to obtain the necessary foreign exchange to pay for their requirements."[1]

The application of the "open-door" principle to colonial trade and of the "free trade" principles to international commerce in general by the means suggested above in Chapter V, should directly remove all the difficulties of *supply*. For example, these principles would prevent the imposition of burdensome duties or other restrictions on raw material exports, which might make it difficult for importing countries to obtain them in sufficient quantities. In particular it would make it impossible for colonial supplies of raw materials to be subjected to export duties or restrictions which discriminated against particular Member States.

There is, however, one question of raw material supplies which needs to be examined in somewhat greater detail. The formation of a monopolistic control over the supplies of a certain raw material may enable the producers of that material to restrict sales and to raise prices in such a way as to obtain a monopoly profit at the expense of the consumers. It may so happen that countries which

---

[1] Cf. League of Nations, *Report of the Committee for the Study of the Problem of Raw Materials*, 1937. (Series of League of Nations Publications. II. Economic and Financial, 1937. II. B. 7), page 11.

consume the greater part of the supplies of the raw material do not control any significant proportion of the territories in which it is produced; and in such a case the consumers will have no political power to ensure that the monopoly is not abused.

The most important—if not the only—examples of monopoly controls are provided by the various international restriction schemes, which have been set up in the case of various products such as rubber, copper and tin to control the production or sales of the commodity. Reference was made to these schemes at the end of Chapter V, where it was suggested that the International Authority should have the power of supervising international cartels in order to ensure that they were not used to raise prices unduly so as to exploit the consumers. There are, however, certain particular problems involved in the case of international schemes for the control of raw material supplies; and while it may be admitted that the control or supervision of such schemes is a very appropriate sphere for action for the International Authority, it is necessary to discuss in more detail on what principles this control should be applied.

There are two possible objectives for such international restriction schemes. In the first place, they may be used to restrict supplies below the level which they would otherwise have reached over an average of good and bad years, in order that prices and the incomes of the producers may be permanently maintained at a higher level. In the second place, such schemes may be employed with the more limited purpose of restricting supplies and maintaining prices in years of bad trade and of increasing supplies and preventing an excessive rise of prices in years of active demand, so that prices and the incomes of producers are little affected on the average of good and bad years but remain at a more stable level. The desire to restrict supplies of certain commodities more or less permanently below the level which they would reach if they were uncontrolled is a natural and in many respects a justifiable one. Changes in technique or the discovery of new sources of supply have in many cases greatly increased the world production of certain raw materials; and other changes in industrial technique have led to the use of substitute materials in certain cases. Such changes have often led to a permanent fall in the price of particular materials; and if—as is often the case—the producers of such materials find it difficult to turn to alternative occupations, the result of the change is liable to be a long transitional period of great poverty and distress among the producers. A restriction scheme which limits the supply by means of a monopolistic agreement may prevent this poverty; and, if it is carried to a sufficient length, may change poverty into riches.

There are, however, serious objections to more or less permanent restriction for these purposes.

The fall in the incomes of the producers which would have occurred if the production of a particular commodity were uncontrolled is a clear indication that, in the changed circumstances, too much labour and capital are employed in the production of the raw material. From the point of view of the interests of the world as a whole it is therefore desirable that some of the labour, capital and natural resources which are utilized for the production of this material should be transferred to other occupations whose products are more highly valued by consumers and where the rewards of labour, capital and natural resources are therefore higher. Indeed, the problem is very similar to that of "special" unemployment, which was discussed above in Chapter V. When any substantial change takes place in economic structure it is probable that certain workers will be no longer needed in their old occupations. Although it is often necessary to take special measures to relieve the temporary distress of such workers, it is also important to make sure that the shift to other expanding industries is not itself prevented.

The grave danger of an international restriction scheme is that by permanently limiting the production of each particular producer of the product in question desirable shifts of workers, capital and natural resources to other occupations may be permanently prevented. Moreover, such schemes may seriously restrict technical progress in the production of the product. It is desirable in the common interest that newly discovered sources of supply should be developed and should supersede the existing sources if the new sources can be worked at a lower cost. But the grant by an international restriction scheme of a certain fixed quota of production to each productive area may prevent this development. There is also a grave danger that those in charge of the restriction scheme will take measures to prevent the use of new technical methods of production which threaten still further to raise the total available supplies of the commodity. To summarize: restriction schemes may maintain more labour, capital and natural resources in the occupation than are really necessary, and may prevent the development of the technically most efficient methods of production at the expense of the consumers of the product; but on the other hand they may help to avoid long transitional periods of distress among the producers.

The application by the International Authority of the various principles outlined in the preceding chapters of this book should ease the process of shifting productive resources from one occupation to another, and should therefore enable the International Authority to insist gradually and without undue distress upon the relaxation of restriction schemes as a permanent method of maintaining the incomes of the producers of raw materials. The gradual application of the principle of free trade, as suggested in Chapter V, will itself extend the demand for various raw materials, which will thereby be able to compete more easily in previously protected markets in which substitute products have been developed or in which uneconomic sources of supply have been opened up. Greater freedom of trade, together with greater freedom of international movements of capital and labour, as suggested in Chapters VI and VIII, would directly ease the process of shifting labour and capital to the production of alternative commodities. By enabling backward areas to increase their industrialization these various changes would also lead to a greater diversification of the products of such territories, and would thus enable such regions to shift from the production of any particular raw material when conditions made such a shift necessary.

International controls of particular raw materials may, however, be used solely to equalize demand as between years of good and of bad trade. Raw materials may be purchased for stock by an international body during years of low prices in order to sell from these stocks to prevent too rapid a rise of prices in other years. Variations are liable to occur in the prices of agricultural products because of variations in crop yields; and the international body may purchase such products for stock during years of abundant crops in order to sell from stock when crop yields are low. Variations in raw material prices may also result from variations in demand. During years of general trade depression the international body controlling any particular product may purchase stocks of that product at relatively low prices in order to sell from these stocks during periods of active trade; but it is to be hoped that the measures discussed in Chapters III and IV will at least mitigate the severity of fluctuations in general trade activity, and that in this way the need for a special policy to stabilize the price of raw materials will be diminished.

The formation of such "buffer" stocks of raw materials by international bodies is not open to the criticisms which were advanced above in the case of more far-reaching schemes of restriction. For the purchase of raw materials at market prices for the formation of a special stock in no way stereotypes the existing methods of production, and does not prevent the more efficient producers from expanding at the expense of the less efficient. Moreover, the operation of such a "buffer" stock does not lead to the permanent maintenance of excess capacity in the production of the raw material, provided that over an average of years the sales from the "buffer" stock in good years are as great as the purchases for the "buffer" stock in bad years. The one danger of such a scheme is, however, that in order to prevent a more or less permanent change in economic conditions from leading to distress among the producers, those in charge of the "buffer" stock will maintain prices above their economic level and will thus be obliged to make continuous additions to the stock. The scheme will work efficiently only if those in charge of the stock set a comparatively low price at which they purchase to add to the stock and are willing ruthlessly to lower this price if more or less permanent changes in economic conditions make it necessary. But for these very reasons the formation of a "buffer" stock alone cannot provide any very far-reaching relief to producers against the special distress which, as we have seen, may follow from a rapid change in technical methods of production.

The above paragraphs illustrate some of the issues which are involved in the choice of an appropriate policy for the regulation of international restriction schemes. It is not possible here to determine exactly what policy should be adopted, but certain general principles may be suggested. International restriction schemes should be submitted to the control and supervision of the International Authority; the interests of the consumers as well as of the producers of the products should be represented on the bodies in control of the various raw materials; and a policy should be adopted which prevents the emergence of the high monopolistic profits or of the permanent rigidities of productive technique which may result from excessive restriction.

The main difficulties of *supply* of raw materials are the imposition of restrictions, prohibitions and duties on the export of raw materials; the failure of some countries adequately to develop their sources of raw materials; and the abuse of international restriction schemes. These difficulties can be removed comparatively easily by the adoption of the measures suggested above. Measures of this kind have already been authoritatively recommended by the Economic Committee of the League of Nations in its report to the Council of the League, dated December 9, 1937:[1]

A. *Prohibitions, Restrictions and Duties on the Export of Raw Materials*

1. Raw materials should not be subjected to any export prohibition or restriction except in pursuance of an international regulation scheme, which is being operated in accordance with the principles set out in Section C below, or some other international agreement between exporting and importing countries.[2]
2. Raw materials should not be subjected to any export duties except duties imposed at a uniform rate irrespective of the country to which the goods are exported either (*a*) for revenue purposes, or (*b*) in order to finance arrangements for improving the production, utilization or marketing of the raw materials in question.

B. *Development of Natural Resources*

Foreigners should have the same rights and facilities as nationals for developing the natural resources both

[1] (Series of League of Nations Publications. II. Economic and Financial, 1937. II. B. 10.)

[2] The terms "prohibition and restriction" in this Section are not of course intended to apply to arrangements for preventing the export of goods of inferior quality or dangerous to health.

of sovereign countries and of colonial territories, subject to their obeying the laws and regulations of the countries concerned.

This principle should be introduced by degrees where it is not already in force, and applied as fully as possible.

It is recognized, however, that provisions may be necessary to regulate the conditions of admission and settlement of foreigners, and also, in colonial territories, to safeguard the interests of the native inhabitants; but such provisions should not be applied in such a way as to neutralize the possibility of foreign participation nor, in colonial territories, to place nationals of the metropolitan country in a privileged position.

C. *International Regulation Schemes relating to the Supply of Raw Materials*

International regulation schemes should be so framed as to admit effective association of consuming interests with their administration, and to make available adequate information regarding their operation. They should be administered in such a way as to provide consumers with adequate supplies of the regulated material, to prevent so far as possible the price of the regulated material from rising to an excessive height and to keep that price reasonably stable.

In so far as Governments are themselves parties to a scheme, they will of course be responsible for seeing that the scheme is framed and administered in accordance with these principles.

The difficulties which some countries have found in making *payment* for raw materials in recent years have, however, been considerably more important than the obstacles to the *supply* of raw materials, to which reference has been made above. Even if abundant supplies of raw materials are available at low prices on the world markets, countries which do not themselves produce raw materials and do not possess colonial territories capable of producing them, will be unable to obtain supplies unless they can obtain foreign money to purchase them. The difficulty which many important countries have recently experienced in obtaining foreign money has given rise to a serious problem of raw materials.

Not only are the difficulties of payment for raw materials more important than the difficulties of supply to which reference has been made above, but the problems of payment are also more complicated and far-reaching from the point of view of finding an appropriate solution for them. The main principle is, however, clear. Some countries find it difficult to obtain raw material supplies because they find it difficult to obtain adequate supplies of foreign money; and they find it difficult to obtain adequate supplies of foreign money because they find it difficult to sell their exports in foreign markets. In other words, a solution of the problem of the balances of payments of these countries on the lines suggested above in Chapter IV and the assurance of greater freedom of international trade by means discussed in Chapters V and VII would themselves solve the problem of payment for raw material imports. This problem is indeed only a special example of the much more general problems of international economic relations which have been discussed in the earlier chapters of this book.

It is, however, frequently argued that countries without colonies are at a special disadvantage because they are obliged to make payment for their purchases of raw materials in foreign currencies; whereas countries possessing colonies in which their own currency is legal tender can purchase their raw material supplies without any foreign money. To what extent does the inclusion of a colonial territory within the monetary area of a particular country ease the problem of payments for colonial raw materials for that country?

In a world in which various national currencies are subjected to strict systems of exchange control, such as those described in Chapter VII, the inclusion of a colonial territory within the monetary area of a particular state may greatly ease the problem of payment for that state; but in a world in which exchange controls did not exist or were limited solely to the prevention of short-term speculative capital movements, the transference of a colonial territory from the currency area of one state to that of another would in itself make no substantial difference. A strict national exchange control would presumably be operated in such a way as to make it more difficult for any colonial territory included in the controlled currency area to purchase supplies from countries outside this area; and the possible lack of adjustment of prices between the area of the controlled currency and outside areas might make it peculiarly difficult for the inhabitants of the colony to sell their products to outside areas. These special obstacles to trade between the colonial territory and other countries outside the currency area would substantially increase the raw material supplies of the country which was applying the currency control. But if, in the absence of exchange control, the rate of exchange between the various currencies was brought into a proper adjustment and there were no special obstacles placed in the way of trade between the colonial territory and any other countries, supplies of raw materials from the colony would not be available on any easier terms to the country whose currency circulated in the colony than to countries with other national currencies.

It is true that a country possessing colonial territories in which its own currency circulates can for a time purchase raw materials from that colony with its notes and without exporting any product in return. But this cannot go on for long; for the continual inflow of notes into the colony would cause an inflationary rise of prices and incomes there, which in turn would lead to a rise in the imports of the colony. In fact, purchases of any country from its colonial territories by means of its own notes must be matched sooner or later by a return flow of these notes to the mother country; and this return flow will take place only in payment for the exports of the mother country. These exports may be sold direct to the colony, or they may be sold to some third country which in turn has obtained the notes from the sale of goods to the colony. In either case, the mother country finances its imports of raw materials from the colony by means of the money obtained from its own exports. The problem of payment for raw material supplies is essentially the problem of finding export markets; and in the absence of the control of trade channels by means of rigid exchange controls, the problem of finding export markets is not substantially affected by transferring a colony from one currency area to another. For these reasons the solution of the problems of international monetary relations and of international trade by the action of the International Authority on the lines suggested in earlier chapters of this book would also solve the problems of payment for raw material supplies.

In addition, the International Authority should ensure—in the interests of the colonies themselves as well as of other countries—that there is an equal opportunity for trade, investment and labour migration for all Member States in the colonial territories; and it should control international restriction schemes for raw materials in such a way as to prevent excessive monopoly prices and undue rigidities in the methods of production employed.

Chapter X

SUMMARY AND CONCLUSIONS

THE preceding chapters have been written in order to suggest a basis upon which a just and efficient system of international economic relations might be built. In doing so certain fundamental principles have been borne in mind. It has been suggested that the main objectives of any such structure should be to prevent serious economic depressions by means of a suitable policy of monetary and economic control, and to increase the freedom with which goods, capital and men may move across national frontiers. But the whole system which has been outlined in the preceding chapters has been devised with the object of permitting Member States with widely divergent internal economic policies and structures to take part in the International Organization. Room has been left for "liberal" economic systems; and an attempt has been made to find place also for "planned" systems. But while planning and state control of economic affairs has in no way been excluded, an attempt has been made to avoid the major danger of such planning —namely, the growth of economic rigidities which

179

prevent the reorganization of industries and the shift of factors of production from occupation to occupation and from district to district, when such shifts are desirable in the interests of total world production.

It may be convenient at this point to summarize briefly the principal suggestions which have been made. In the monetary sphere it is suggested that an International Bank should be instituted with the right of note issue, and that it should contract or expand this issue in order to help national monetary policies designed to offset booms or depressions of trade activity. The Member States would preserve their own national currencies, which would be pegged at given values in terms of the notes of the International Bank; but the rates at which these national currencies were pegged would be altered from time to time in such a way as to preserve equilibrium in the balances of payments of the various Member States. The International Bank would also operate an international exchange equalization fund in order to offset speculative movements of short-term capital, and it would organize a market in forward exchanges in order to reduce the financial risks of international trade. The Member States would be permitted to maintain complete systems of foreign exchange control, provided that these controls were employed only to prevent short-term capital movements.

In so far as international trade is concerned,

the International Authority would arrange for the gradual reduction of barriers to trade—such as tariffs, quotas, prohibitions, controls over the purchase of foreign exchange for the finance of imports, and bilateral clearing agreements. Member States with planned economies would be permitted to control their foreign trade provided that imports and exports were planned on the principles of buying in the cheapest and selling in the dearest market. The International Authority would also have control over international cartels and restriction schemes, and over national import and export boards, to ensure that similar principles of operation were observed.

International capital movements—except in the case of speculative movements of short-term capital—would be freed from restrictions; and the International Authority might constitute a special international commission to ensure this, and to preserve the "open-door" for capital investment in colonial territories. International movements of population would also be subjected to the control of the International Authority, and greater freedom of migration would be allowed. Subject to various modifications due to non-economic considerations, greater freedom of immigration would be allowed into countries in which a population decline was threatened; and on the other hand restrictions on emigration might be imposed in the case of countries in which the internal growth of population was excessive and uncontrolled.

There are, however, a number of particular economic problems which have not been discussed in the preceding chapters, either because they are of secondary importance or else because their solution depends essentially upon political rather than economic considerations. For example, the International Authority will presumably be responsible for determining the basis of economic relations with the states which do not become members of the International Organization. This question is primarily a political one. It might, for example, be decided to impose an import duty of any given level upon all the imports from all the countries outside the International Organization. Such an arrangement might provide an incentive for the outside states to join the International Organization; and it might give an additional economic coherence to the Organization itself, in addition to providing a source of revenue. The principle might be still further extended by partially or wholly closing the area under the control of the International Authority to migration and capital investment by outside states. Alternatively, it might be decided to treat outside states from the economic point of view as far as possible in the same way as the Member States, and to apply a policy of free trade, and of freedom of movement for labour and capital between the Member States and other countries. Such a policy might be calculated to raise the general standard of living as high as possible, to set an example, and to prevent economic conflicts with the outside world. As a third possibility, the International Authority might use the weapons of restrictions of trade, and of movements of capital and labour from outside states as a means of economic bargaining; and by individual agreements with the various countries concerned it might attempt to obtain the most favourable treatment possible for the Member States.

Another set of problems which has not been examined in this book and which depends for its solution primarily upon non-economic considerations is raised by the necessity of providing the International Authority with a revenue. The solution of this problem would depend very largely upon the scope of the non-economic functions which were handed over to the International Authority. If, for example, it were entrusted with the whole of the armed forces of the Member States or with other extensive functions, it would need to be endowed with the power of raising a tax revenue directly for its own purposes. This would in turn raise complicated questions relating to the division of different taxing powers between the national governments of the Member States and the International Authority itself—questions which are comparable to those already raised in existing federal states. If, on the other hand, the International Authority were entrusted only with limited technical functions, such as the economic functions discussed in this book, it is probable that its revenue could be assured by contributions from the governments of the Member States, comparable to the contributions made by the states which are members of the League of Nations.

If the functions of the International Authority are at all extensive, it will need a relatively large revenue; and the raising of this revenue, whether it be effected by means of taxation imposed by the International Authority directly or by means of contributions from the governments of the Member States, will involve the question of assessing the burden as between rich and poor states. The raising of such a revenue will give rise immediately to the possibility of reducing the inequalities of income as between the various Member States by a system of progressive taxation or state contributions which imposes the largest *per capita* burden on the Member States with the highest *per capita* real income. It is, however, difficult to devise reliable indices to measure the difference between the level of real incomes in different countries; and this question involves technical difficulties and complexities which it is not possible to discuss at length in this book.

The problem of international inequalities of real income is, however, an important one which has been treated only incidentally in the course of this book. In addition to the use of progressive taxes or state contributions to the International Authority as a means of reducing such inequalities, the expenditure of its revenue by the International Authority might be used for the same purpose. This possibility also depends very largely upon non-economic considerations; for it is only if the International Authority is endowed with extensive social, medical or educational functions that it can hope to diminish international inequalities by concentrating such expenditure mainly on the poorer states.

Various suggestions have, however, been made incidentally in the course of this book which would help to meet the problem of international inequalities. It has already been observed that greater freedom of trade and of international capital movements would probably help to raise the standard of living of the more backward countries nearer to the standard of the more advanced countries; for it would enable the backward countries to share in the advantages of industrialization and of large-scale production. Migration of labour from countries with low wages to countries with high wages would also diminish international inequalities. Finally, in agriculture, mining and industry the improvement of technical methods of production in the less advanced regions of the world towards the standards of the most advanced countries would not only greatly increase total world production, but would much diminish the existing wide inequalities as between the different regions of the world. It is possible that the International Authority would make its most effective contribution towards the diminution of international inequalities by setting up a special commission charged with the generalization of advanced technical knowledge throughout the Member States.

If the International Organization is constituted at the termination of the present war, it will be faced immediately with peculiarly difficult circumstances in which to apply the various economic principles which have been suggested in the preceding chapters of this book. The transition from war to peace conditions will raise problems of a special complexity. As far as it is possible to judge from the experience of economic events after the war of 1914–18, demobilization is likely to lead to an abrupt increase in the number of persons seeking work, while at the same time the cessation of government expenditure for munitions and other war orders is likely to lead to a slump in total demand. This post-war slump and unemployment may be delayed, as it was in many countries after 1914–18, by an immediate post-war boom due to the need for civil reconstruction and to civil orders to undertake works which were postponed during the war.

For these reasons the International Authority may have to start its career at a time peculiarly liable to violent fluctuations in trade activity. In order to help the various Member States to mitigate or to prevent these fluctuations, the International Bank should be prepared to make bold use of its powers of control over the total monetary reserves of the central banks of the Member States—restricting these supplies during the boom and expanding them extensively and without hesitation during the slump. If the International Authority is endowed with extensive functions, which involve the expenditure of significant sums of money, it should time this expenditure as far as possible with a view to offsetting the fluctuations in other demands. For example, if it were entrusted with the control of international communications it should plan its capital expenditure upon the reconstruction and development of railways and shipping so that it could be undertaken as far as possible during periods of bad trade and general unemployment. Or if it were entrusted with control over international loans raised for the rebuilding of devastated areas, such control might be used to time these expenditures so as to offset the fluctuations in general trade activity. In any case the International Authority should encourage the Member States to co-operate in order to co-ordinate their internal monetary policies and to time their internal expenditures on public works in such a way as to diminish the severity of any post-war slump.

At the end of the war it will become necessary to restore economic relations between enemy states. The level of prices and costs in the various belligerent states may have moved in very divergent ways in the course of the war; and blockades which have separated various markets may have led to great divergences in the relation between the prices of particular products in the various national markets. In view of these developments it will be particularly desirable to have the services of an international body to adjust the exchange rates between the various national currencies on the principles suggested in Chapter IV, in order to bring the balances of payments of the different states into equilibrium. But while this part of the work of the International Authority will be particularly valuable immediately after the war, it will—for the very same reasons —be particularly difficult.

To judge from the experience of the period after the war of 1914–18, the post-war period will bring with it serious problems of "special" unemployment. Certain industries — in particular those which produce armaments—will be overdeveloped from the point of view of the requirements of peace. In some countries various industries may have grown up as a result of blockades which have prevented the import of commodities from the normal foreign sources. The termination of hostilities may threaten such industries with a serious problem of "special" unemployment. For these reasons the function of the International Authority in reducing barriers to international trade may be a peculiarly delicate one immediately after the war; for the natural reaction of national states may be to mitigate these problems of "special" unemployment by protecting the industries concerned from foreign competition. In view of these possibilities it may be wise for the International Authority to attempt to distinguish between two types of products—those for which the demand is stimulated by war conditions and those for which the demand is greater in peace-time; and reductions of tariffs and other trade barriers might at first be concentrated upon the second type of commodity.

For similar reasons it is probable that the International Authority should suspend, during the period of any serious post-war slump, the measures which it was taking for the reduction of trade barriers, and should be content during such a period with preventing the growth of fresh barriers to trade. For it is naturally much easier to effect a reduction in trade barriers when the general demand for goods and services is growing than during a period of shrinking markets and of growing unemployment. When effective measures have been taken to stimulate the total volume of monetary demand in order to overcome any post-war slump, the policy of reducing trade barriers might be again effectively prosecuted.

In its supervision of international capital movements the International Authority will probably have special functions to perform immediately after the war. International loans for financial and economic reconstruction may become very important in order to rehabilitate the poorer countries or the countries which have suffered most from the war. It has already been argued in Chapter VI that the payment of interest and sinking fund on foreign loans can only be ensured if certain conditions are fulfilled, among which are the existence of an efficient mechanism for the readjustment of the balances of international payments of the countries concerned and the institution of a regime of comparatively free international trade. For this reason substantial reconstruction loans should probably only be granted as between Member States, which have accepted these economic conditions as a part of the International Organization. In this case the International Authority might appropriately organize and control such reconstruction loans; and the grant of such loans might in itself provide a powerful incentive for the states in need of them to join the International Organization.

For these reasons the International Organization would be specially needed directly after the war. If it could deal at all effectively with the peculiarly difficult economic problems of the immediate post-war period, it would have established a sound and popular basis on which to construct its permanent work of meeting the less rapid adjustments needed in more normal times. The object of this book has been to contribute towards the choice of just and efficient principles upon which such a durable system of international economic relations may be built.

Index

191